STEP-BY-STEP

Town Gardens

STEP-BY-STEP

Town Gardens

Valerie Bradley

INDEX

First published in 1998 by Lorenz Books

© 1998 Anness Publishing Limited

Lorenz Books is an imprint of
Anness Publishing Limited
Hermes House
88-89 Blackfriars Road
London SE1 8HA

This edition published in 1998 for Index

ISBN 1 85967 586 7

A CIP catalogue record is available from the British Library

Publisher: Joanna Lorenz
Senior Editor: Lindsay Porter
Designer: Caroline Reeves

Printed in Hong Kong

1 3 5 7 9 10 8 6 4 2

CONTENTS

INTRODUCTION

With the price of land in towns at a premium, most city dwellers
are lucky to have an outdoor space of any description, whether a
private garden, a tiny patio or simply a balcony. This is not so much
a handicap as a challenge: in fact, a great deal can be done to create
a little patch of Eden in such confined spaces. There is a plant for any
situation, no matter how inhospitable the site might appear to be, and,
with the right selection, even a dark, drab, concrete-covered front yard
can be completely transformed into a pretty, welcoming sight
throughout the year.

Colour can be used in many ways, to create different moods within the
garden, both with plants and with the accessories that accompany them.
Brick or concrete act as a plain foil to a dramatic planting scheme, and
the plants themselves can be selected to set the tone of the area.
Furniture and pots can all be painted in colours that will complement
or contrast with the plants, particularly around an outdoor seating area
and where lots of containers are being used together.

The greatest advantage of having a garden is that it extends the living
space to the maximum, and this applies equally to a balcony, or even
a window box. Sitting surrounded by nature provides the most
wonderful release from the stresses and strains at the end of a busy
day's work. This book will help you to make the most of your
garden space – no matter how small.

Opposite: *A small patio area and
collection of planted containers can be
incorporated into most gardens, no
matter what the size or location.*

THE FRONT GARDEN

Although not always the easiest part of the garden to maintain, the area at the front of the house is an important focal point, providing a welcome to visitors and family. No matter how limited the space, pots, hanging baskets and shrubs can all create a cheerful impression.

This area presents particular challenges in the city. The site is constantly exposed to urban influences, such as pollution, and it will most likely be dry because of the proximity of walls or buildings. Moreover, although the impression given by the front is important, most people have limited time for maintenance and want to concentrate their effort on the areas they use most – usually the back garden. The front garden needs to carry on looking good with the minimum of attention, and careful choice of plants for the front can solve all of these problems.

Opposite: *Although you may spend less time in the area at the front of the house, plants growing by the door, positioned up stairs and under windows will create a welcoming impression.*

Access to the Front Garden

Make allowances for the need to get to key places within the design and there should be no need for anyone ever to walk on a border.

PRACTICAL PLANNING

At the front of any building, there is always a question of access. While a straight line from the gate to the door may be uninteresting, any attempt to deviate from it may cause less interested visitors to continue to walk on the same line as usual and trample the planting. If there is room, a straight path can be broken up by placing a large object, such as a sun-dial or birdbath, in the middle, and running the path in a circular pattern around each side of it, so that the deviation from the original line is minimal and the option is open to pass on either side of the ornament.

It is usually more practical to accept the need for a straight path, and work around it; it can soon be given added interest, by softening the edges with low-growing, spreading plants which will tolerate being stepped on.

DESIGNING THE GARDEN

1 Draw the outline of the garden with the position of the house and other features. Don't forget to include items such as bins (trash cans) or storage areas. Access is a key consideration.

2 If you have a drawing board, use tracing paper overlays for your roughs while experimenting with ideas. If the garden is very small, you may be able simply to attach the plan to a clipboard.

3 Film and pens of the type used for overhead projection are effective if you prefer to use colours that can be wiped off for easy correction.

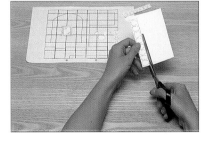

4 You may find it helpful to use visual aids that can be moved around when designing. Draw and cut out features to scale such as raised beds etc. These can be moved around until you are happy with the design.

Above: *This garden makes the most of a small square area by combining plants with paving.*

Opposite: *A path leading to the front steps is softened by a colourful border.*

Planting for the Front Garden

There is a range of plants for every situation, be it dry or wet, hot or cold, sunny or shady. With a little thought, it will usually be possible to find plants to provide colour or interest for every month of the year, so that the garden need never look dull.

Above: Lysimachia nummularia 'Aurea' is ideal for use as ground cover, either growing to soften the edges of paths or planted among paving.

Above: Pulmonaria saccharata *is recommended as a ground cover plant and can be mixed with bulbs and perennials for seasonal interest.*

PLANTING PLAN

It is important to bear in mind the ultimate size of plants, especially if the area is not large. If a plant becomes too big it will dominate the growing area, crowding out its companions and depriving them of water, light and nutrients. Positioned too near the building, it will also block light from the windows, and may interfere with paths and drains. However, there are thousands of plants that are suited to different light levels and soil types, and that will remain small or medium-sized, and many more that are slightly larger but that can be kept under control by a regular pruning regime.

Where the garden is open (as opposed to enclosed by a wall or fence), plants can be used to define boundaries and discourage trespassing, without creating a solid barrier. Where noise is a problem, however, a solid barrier may be exactly the solution to baffle the sound and deflect it up over the house.

Containers make a dramatic impact at the front of a house, not least because they can be changed regularly to provide a constant display of colour or foliage; wall-shrubs will add another dimension, particularly if they have flowering climbing plants growing through them to extend the season of interest.

Left: Hypericum *'Hidcote' will grow successfully in an east-facing garden.*

Above: *Planting on steps will create interest at different levels and has the advantage of softening hard lines.*

Ground-covering Plants

Plants which do not exceed 45cm (18in) in height are often referred to as "ground cover", particularly when they have a spreading habit and can be used as a means of softening and disguising hard edges or straight lines.

LOW-MAINTENANCE SOLUTIONS

Low-growing and ground-covering plants are useful for the city front garden in a number of ways, both in the garden and around its edges. They are ideal for softening the edges of a path when they are allowed to grow partly on to the hard surface, and they can be dotted in planting holes left among the slabs, to break up a large expanse of paving. If you have borders in the front garden, ground-cover plants fill and soften the front of the border and will soon fill all gaps. This, in turn, helps to suppress weeds, because, in common with most other seedlings, weeds need light to grow. Eliminating the need to cultivate the soil to get rid of weeds will also help prevent more weeds from appearing, as no more seeds are brought to the surface. Thus ground cover is ideal for the city garden, as it is low-maintenance.

Another bonus is that a covering of leaves over the surface of the soil reduces the amount of water lost to evaporation on a warm or windy day. The soil is kept moist and the amount of water needed to keep the other plants alive is reduced.

Many of the plants used as ground cover are quite tough, and require little in the way of maintenance after planting. *Hypericum calycinum*, for instance, simply needs annual clipping with a strimmer (string-line trimmer), to reduce the height and encourage bushiness. Other than that, an annual feed will suffice for it to thrive.

Thus, when the amount of time available for maintenance is limited, as it often is for city gardens, using a low covering of plants can reduce the necessary work quite considerably, while still providing a welcoming entrance to your home.

LOW-GROWING AND GROUND-COVERING PLANTS

Ajuga reptans
Anaphalis triplinervis
Aubrieta deltoidea
Bergenia cordifolia
Campanula carpatica
Epimedium x *youngianum*
  'Niveum'
Erigeron karvinskianus
Geranium sanguineum
Hedera colchica

Helianthemum nummularium
  x *Heucherella tiarelloides*
Hosta sieboldiana
Hypericum calycinum
Lysimachia nummularia
Pachysandra terminalis
Pulmonaria saccherata
Rosa 'Max Graf'
Saxifraga cuneifolia
Tiarella cordifolia
Vinca minor

PLANTING GROUND COVER

1 To plant ground cover, clear the ground of weeds first. Annual weeds can be hoed off or killed with a herbicide. Some perennial weeds will have to be dug out by hand.

2 Fork in as much rotted manure or garden compost as you can spare, then apply a slow-release or controlled-release fertilizer and rake it in lightly.

3 Unless your ground cover spreads by underground stems it is best to plant through a mulching sheet to control weeds while the plants are becoming established. Cut a cross where the plant is to be positioned.

4 Plant in staggered rows, planting small plants through the slits with a trowel. Water thoroughly after planting, and in dry weather throughout the first year.

5 Until the plants have grown together you may want to use a decorative mulch such as chipped bark to improve the appearance.

Dry Areas

Most gardens have patches where, for whatever reason, there is less moisture than elsewhere. This is especially a problem in front gardens, which are often overhung by buildings and other structures that create "rain shadows". If you improve the soil and select plants that enjoy dry conditions, however, this need not be a problem. Factors that can influence the amount of moisture within the garden include rainfall, sunshine, soil type, drainage, surrounding structures and the plants already in position.

RETAINING MOISTURE

Rainfall can vary considerably within quite small areas depending on local topographical conditions; this can result in dramatically different amounts of water reaching the soil in different parts of the garden. The direction in which the garden faces can affect the water it receives if the house is positioned as a shield. Even though plenty of rain falls, it may not be falling on the soil where it is needed, but on the house, where it runs off down the drains.

How long the moisture is held within the soil, and therefore how long it is available for use by the plants, is affected by both the amount of sun and shade and the soil type. A light, sandy soil loses its moisture quickly, because there are large air spaces between the particles, allowing rapid drainage. A heavy, clay soil, on the other hand, has only tiny air spaces, because the soil particles are much smaller. The water is slower to drain away and is therefore available to the plants for a longer time.

Drainage will also be affected by the angle of the garden, in that a flat area will take longer to drain than one that slopes.

Having large, established specimens already *in situ* can mean that there is less water available for newly introduced plants. An older plant will have sent roots down to the lower levels within the soil, to take advantage of all the moisture it can, leaving little for the new plant that is still reliant on water much nearer the surface. A five-year-old tree, for example, will take up in excess of 4 litres (1 gallon) of water every day.

If the garden does not receive enough rainfall to support plants with this kind of requirement, you may have to consider choosing plants that need a lower intake. One way to improve moisture is by adding a mulch around the base of the plants. This keeps the soil moist by slowing down evaporation.

Above: Salvia officinalis *will grow successfully in dry soil.*

1 Prepare the ground thoroughly, digging it over and working in plenty of organic material such as rotted manure or garden compost if the soil is impoverished.

2 Loose mulches will control annual weeds and prevent new perennial ones from starting. Dig up deep-rooted perennial weeds, otherwise they could grow through the mulch.

3 Water the ground thoroughly before applying the mulch. Do not apply a mulch to dry ground.

4 Spread the mulch thickly. This is bark mulch, but there are many other decorative mulches available.

PLANTS FOR DRY SITUATIONS

Agapanthus
Aster novi-belgii 'Jenny'
Buddleja alternifolia
Campanula persicifolia
Convolvulus cneorum
Cortaderia selloana
  'Aureolineata'
Corylus avellana 'Contorta'
Cytisus battandieri
Diascia fetcaniensis
Eryngium bourgatii
Escallonia 'Slieve Donard'
Gaultonia candicans
x *Halimiocistus wintonensis*
Lavandula angustifolia
Liriope muscari
Osteospermum 'Buttermilk'
Papaver orientale 'Mrs Perry'
Salvia officinalis
Senecio 'Sunshine'
Yucca filamentosa

Above: Lavendula *'Hidcote'* prefers dry soil.

Right: *Gardening in containers is one way to overcome less-than-perfect soil types, and will allow you to grow certain species that might not normally flourish in your garden.*

Aspect

The aspect of the front garden is something you don't have any choice about. Also, because of the primary need to make it an efficient access area, you may not have much scope for altering where blocks of planting or containers are positioned. Whichever direction the garden faces, though, there will be a range of plants suitable for growing in it; selecting the right plants will produce a wonderful show of colour throughout the year.

KNOW YOUR PLANTS

The direction the garden faces will have a strong influence on the plants likely to thrive in it. If a plant originally hails from the warm, dry and sunny countries that border the Mediterranean, it is unlikely to grow well in a damp, shady corner, and, similarly, a bog plant from a northern forest will not enjoy being placed between a south-facing wall and a path. One of the basic keys to successful gardening is to match the position and the plant as closely as possible. Doing this when the plant is first acquired will save both time and money, because the plant will not have to be dug up later when it has failed to thrive and most of the growing season has been lost. A good nursery is invaluable for advice, but most plants will be labelled.

PLANTS FOR EAST-FACING POSITIONS

Berberis darwinii
Bergenia cordifolia
Chaenomeles x *superba*
Clematis montana
Clematis tangutica
Cotoneaster horizontalis
Deutzia scabra
Dodecatheon meadia
Euphorbia griffithii
Forsythia suspensa
Galanthus nivalis (snowdrop)
Hamamelis mollis (witch hazel)
Helleborus foetidus
Hypericum 'Hidcote'
Lonicera periclymenum
Pyracantha 'Golden Glow'
Rosa rugosa
Vinca major (periwinkle)

PLANTS FOR NORTH-FACING POSITIONS

Akebia quinata
Berberis x *stenophylla*
Camellia japonica
Camellia x *williamsii*
Clematis alpina
Clematis 'Nelly Moser'
Choisya ternata
Crinodendron hookerianum
Eriobotrya japonica
Euonymus fortunei
Garrya elliptica
Hedera colchica
Hedera helix
Hydrangea petiolaris
Ilex corallina
Jasminum nudiflorum
Kerria japonica 'Pleniflora'
Mahonia japonica
Parthenocissus
Piptanthus laburnifolius
Tropaeolum speciosum

Above: Choisya ternata *'Sundance'.*

Right: Parthenocissus *is suitable for a north-facing garden. A good nursery will give advice on the best plants for your garden.*

Left: Echinops bannaticus *provides a splash of colour in a south-facing garden.*

Right: *For plants to thrive, choose those suitable for the garden's aspect. There is little chance of a shade-loving hosta flourishing in a sunny south-facing garden.*

PLANTS FOR SOUTH-FACING POSITIONS

Aethionema grandiflorum
Campsis x *tagliabuana*
 'Madame Galen'
Canna indica
Cistus x *pulverulentus* 'Sunset'
Dianthus
Dryas octopetala
Eccremocarpus scaber
Echinacea purpurea
Echinops ritro
Fritillaria imperialis

Geranium cinereum
 'Ballerina'
Helenium 'Waldtraut'
Imperata cylindrica
 'Red Baron'
Lilium lancifolium
Moluccella laevis
Osteospermum 'Whirligig'
Reseda odorata
Salvia officinalis 'Tricolor'
Sempervivum arachnoideum
Senecio 'Sunshine'

PLANTS FOR WEST-FACING POSITIONS

Abelia x *grandiflora*
Campsis radicans
Ceanothus 'Gloire de Versailles'
Ceanothus impressus
Cistus x *cyprius*
Crocosmia cultivars
Deutzia scabra 'Plena'
Eccremocarpus scaber
Fremontodendron
 'California Glory'
Geranium 'Johnson's Blue'
Helichrysum italicum

Humulus lupulus 'Aureus'
Ipomoea hederacea
Kolkwitzia amabilis
Lavandula angustifolia
 'Hidcote'
Lavandula stoechas
Papaver orientale
Penstemon cultivars
Rosmarinus officinalis
 (rosemary)
Vitis coignetiae

Above: *Ideal for south-facing gardens,* Helenium 'Waldraut' *will also tolerate very alkaline soil.*

Above: Campsis radicans *is an ideal screening plant.*

Right: *Growing plants in pots will allow you to move them into full sun or shade easily.*

Choosing Plants to Cope with Pollution

Pollution of one sort or another is a problem in all areas but town gardens are particularly exposed to its effects because of their location in centres of population, commerce and manufacturing. In this battle between our need for the peace and tranquillity of nature and the necessities of economic activity, the front garden is the front line. Some plants can cope with the problems of pollution, while others cannot, but with thoughtful planting, the garden need look no less beautiful in a town than in the middle of the countryside.

POLLUTION-TOLERANT PLANTS

Amelanchier canadensis	*Garrya* (all)
Aucuba japonica	*Ilex aquifolium* and cultivars
Berberis (all)	*Leycesteria formosa*
Buddleja davidii	*Ligustrum ovalifolium*
Ceratostigma willmottianum	*Olearia* x *haastii*
Chaenomeles (all)	x *Osmarea burkwoodii*
Cotoneaster (most)	*Philadelphus* (all)
Elaeagnus x *ebbingei*	*Syringa* (all)
Elaeagnus pungens and cultivars	*Tamarix tetrandra*
Forsythia (all)	*Weigela florida*

PROBLEM SITES

Any substance in the atmosphere that is not beneficial can constitute pollution, whether it is air-borne, water-borne or deposited directly. Some plants are more tolerant of pollution than others and it is worth knowing which these are.

The most obvious site at risk from pollution is next to a busy main road, where traffic is constantly streaming past or snarled up in slow-moving jams. Not only does the deposit from the vehicle exhausts settle on the leaves throughout the year but, if the road is salted in winter, it is splashed on to the nearest plants as the traffic passes. The solution may be as simple as a hedge of plants that can tolerate this kind of treatment, planted along the most vulnerable part of the garden to protect the more delicate species behind it.

Environmental pollution is a much more general problem to the garden. In an area with such difficulties it is worth choosing a selection of plants that are known to be tolerant of a range of unfavourable conditions. Careful selection will provide a varied collection of both evergreen and deciduous plants, for flowers and foliage, that will provide interest throughout the year.

Left: Ilex *(holly) will tolerate most urban conditions.*

Right: Berberis *can be planted to shield more delicate plants.*

Opposite: *Plants at the front of the house often have to contend with car exhaust. By choosing plants that are tolerant of such conditions, you can achieve gardening success.*

Repelling Unwanted Visitors

In the absence of a drawbridge, it is sometimes difficult to avoid having trespassers on the garden, whether they have two legs, four or even six. Measures can be taken to make the garden a less inviting prospect for invaders, without spoiling its pleasant overall appearance.

ANIMALS AND INSECTS

Neither animals nor insects recognize human boundaries, and if something looks or smells interesting to them, they will investigate. This can result in damage to plants. Although there isn't an instant solution, there are steps that you can take without resorting to chemicals.

Certain plants attract animals; they are usually plants with strong odours, such as *Nepeta* x *faassenii* (catmint), so avoiding these will reduce the attraction of your garden.

Ants are a particular nuisance in the garden because, although they do not directly damage plants, they tunnel through the soil along the lines already created by the roots, causing the root to lose contact with the soil and dry out. If this happens along enough roots, the plant can no longer take up the water it needs to live, and it will die. Higher up on the plant, ants "farm" aphids (greenfly), which feed on sap from the leaves causing distorted foliage and poor growth, in order to take advantage of the sweet honeydew aphids excrete. Ant-repellant plants such as pennyroyal *(Mentha pulegium)* can be used around the base of subjects which are particularly prone to attack.

Once the garden is established, the best means of controlling insect pests is to encourage other insects that act as predators.

Above: *Climbing roses are a decorative and practical way to discourage unwelcome visitors from scaling fences to gain access to the garden.*

Below left: *Prickly plants will deter both human and animal visitors to the garden.*

PRACTICAL WAYS TO PREVENT THEFT AND DAMAGE

- Put a brick in the base of a container, making it too heavy to move easily.

- Use a tree anchor (saves using a stake).

- Fit small hanging-basket locks to protect your baskets.

- Install security lighting.

- Photograph valuable plants and ornaments.

PRICKLY OR THORNY PLANTS

Aralia spinosus
Berberis julianae
Berberis x *stenophylla*
Chaenomeles speciosa
Colletia spinosissima
Crataegus monogyna
Elaeagnus angustifolia
  'Oleaster'
Ilex x *altaclarensis*
  'Golden King'
Ilex aquifolium
  'Ferox argentea'
Ilex aquifolium 'Silver Queen'
Mahonia aquifolium
  'Atropurpurea'
Mahonia x *media* 'Charity'
Osmanthus heterophyllus
Poncirus trifoliata
Pyracantha 'Mohave'
Ribes speciosum
Robinia hispida
Rosa rugosa
Rubus tricolor
Smilax biflora

PROBLEMS WITH HUMAN VISITORS

People visit the garden for many reasons and tailoring the design in response to these reasons will welcome those who visit for pleasure, help those who visit through necessity and discourage those who have less beneficent motives.

People can cause damage to the garden in many ways, often without even realizing it. Simply walking across a frost-covered lawn will damage the frozen cells of the grass plants, leaving a trail of brown footprints which will take most of the spring to fade. This can be overcome by using the planting to guide the visitor to the proper point of access – a hedge, even a low one, acts as a physical barrier and will cause people to detour around it.

Less easy to deal with is the visitor with less than honest intentions, but remember that most theft is opportunistic rather than premeditated, and reducing the number of easily-carried-away items on view should have an effect on this. Tools, for instance, should be tidied away if the garden is left unattended. Prickly or thorny plants are an effective deterrent near a potential point of entry, perhaps against a wall that could be scaled, but don't plant anything large enough to screen the door as this may allow someone enough time to try the lock. To this end, security lighting which comes on automatically is also effective.

Right: *Tall fences maintain privacy and discourage access to the garden and can be softened with climbing plants.*

Reducing Noise

While it is difficult to eliminate an annoying noise completely, it is possible to use plants to filter it down to a more acceptable level. Plants near the house look much more attractive than sound-proofing.

HEDGES AS SCREENING

The one thing it is difficult to get away from in a built-up area is noise – it is constant, from traffic, trains, aircraft, people and so on. To a large extent, noise becomes so familiar that it barely registers, but there are occasions when it is preferable to do something about it. At the front of a house, a particularly persistent noise may interfere with sleeping, for instance, and here it may be useful to install plants to act as a baffle to the noise and to try to deflect it up over the building.

Hedges, particularly when they consist of broad-leaved evergreen plants such as *Prunus laurocerasus, Aucuba japonica* or *Elaeagnus* x *ebbingei*, are effective at reducing noise, because they form a dense barrier throughout the year. The higher the hedge, the higher it will deflect the noise.

In a very small garden, this may not be an option, because hedges do take up quite a lot of space, so the strategic positioning of a single upright or small-sized tree may be necessary. Both *Prunus* 'Amanogawa' (upright) and *Prunus* x *subhirtella* 'Autumnalis' (a small tree bearing flowers throughout the autumn and winter) are deciduous trees suitable for small gardens.

Left: *This planted trough, positioned on a roof, provides an element of screening from noises nearby.*

Above: *A dense planting of tall shrubs can act as an effective screen against noise, as well as providing privacy from nearby houses or roads.*

PLANTING A HEDGE

1 Mark out the line of the hedge with a string and canes. Use a spade to dig holes deep enough to accommodate the plants' roots, allowing space for the intended thickness of the hedge. For each hole, place the rootball against the side of the hole, and cover with soil.

2 Firm the soil gently with your foot. Repeat until the whole row has been planted; then apply a dressing of fertilizer on to the soil surface around the young plants and fork this into the top 5cm (2in) of soil.

3 Water the plants in well, then add a layer of organic matter 10cm (4in) deep as a mulch over the soil surface, to retain moisture and suppress weeds.

Above: *If you have the space for a hedge, it will provide a natural barrier from noise and activity beyond. While a young hedge is growing to maturity, you can create other screening options with trellises, fences or tall herbaceous plants.*

THE BACK GARDEN

While the front garden is generally on display, in the private part of the garden at the back of the house, your imagination can take over. In this secret haven, all the stresses and cares of the day are put aside in favour of pleasure and relaxation.

No matter what size it is, even the tiniest patch can be filled with plants to delight the senses. The size of the garden is of little importance to the end result, because, by considering scale and colour carefully, and using every surface and dimension to the full, you can create an impression that the garden is much bigger, longer or wider than it really is.

Much more critical to success are the basic steps that will ensure the plants grow well. The pH of the soil – how acidic or alkaline it is – will govern the range of plants to an extent, as well as the general aspect of the garden and amount of sun it receives. By taking all these factors into account, you will discover ways to create the perfect garden no matter how restricting the site might at first appear.

Opposite: *In most cities, back gardens are small and shady, but these factors need not restrict the garden's potential.*

Access to the Back Garden

Making sure that the routes to certain points around the garden are kept clear will reduce the risk of damage to the plants, but this does not have to mean having a straight concrete path down the middle.

PRACTICAL PLANNING

The back garden can have such a multitude of uses that the points for access are many and varied, and are seldom as simple as just in-and-out. There may be a back gate, for reaching a rubbish (trash) storage area or garage; a shed, compost heap or greenhouse; a clothes line; or a children's play area, all of which will need a direct line of access. Not providing this direct route will result in "desire lines" being worn across the lawn or through the plants as short-cuts are inevitably taken. Watching these lines develop is often the easiest way of working out exactly where the paths ought to go, but by then, the damage may have been done.

There are many different surfaces to choose from for paths, from bark to stone, brick to gravel, and the choice is entirely personal. Aim to keep the surface material in context with the house wherever possible. Match the brick to those used on the house or select a complementary shade of gravel.

If the path runs across, or next to, a lawn, it is important to remember that loose gravel will seriously damage the blades of a lawnmower. Unless the gravel can be resin-bonded to keep it in place, it is probably better to go for slabs or bricks, which can be set lower than the grass, or bark, which is softer and will not cause so much damage.

Right: *When planning seating areas, consider where the access routes will lead across the garden.*

Below: *A winding path leads the visitor through the garden past points of interest.*

Above: *Paving stones surrounded by ground-cover plants form a practical and decorative surface for a garden path.*

Opposite: *Steps leading from the house and patio area to the rest of the garden are softened with pots and containers.*

Designing the Back Garden to Suit You

Having an overall plan in mind for the garden does not mean having to create an artistic masterpiece on paper. Garden design is entirely personal and depends on the garden, its uses and its owners – using a rough plan simply helps to keep things in perspective.

ASSESS YOUR NEEDS

Gardens come in all shapes and sizes and no two will ever look alike, especially once the plants are in place. How it is designed will depend on its intended use and the amount of time you want to spend maintaining it.

Where the garden belongs to a couple, or a single person, there is larger scope in the choice of plants. In a family garden, however, the plants have to be altogether more robust. Safety is also a priority where there are children; plants that bear thorns and prickles should be kept away from play areas. If the size of garden allows, create an area for the children to play where the plants are safe, resilient and easily pruned back, allowing the rest of the garden to be filled with more choice species.

Tailor the level of maintenance to suit your needs. If you don't have a lot of time, make use of mulches and ground-covering plants to smother weeds and conserve moisture for a low-upkeep regime.

Remember too, in a small garden, every plant should earn its place by providing a good display at least once, and preferably twice through the year.

CIRCULAR THEME

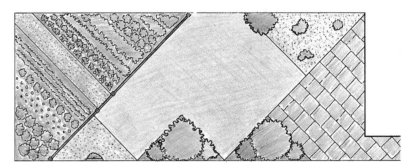

DIAGONAL THEME

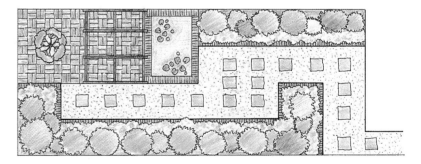

RECTANGULAR THEME

Above: *Three garden designs based on a long, rectangular plot.*

Left: *Pots and containers are ideal in a small space, and can be rearranged easily if you would like a change.*

Opposite: *It is often possible to accommodate a water feature in the smallest garden. This will add an extra dimension to the planting scheme.*

Deceiving the Eye

No garden is ever the exact shape the owner wants, but this need not be a problem because planting and accessories can be used very effectively to change one's perception of shape and distance. If the garden is particularly long and thin, or wide but shallow, it may be desirable to use a little bit of trickery to make it look different.

OPTICAL ILLUSIONS

Although there are limits to how much you can change the site physically, you can learn some optical tricks to adjust its appearance visually.

A long, straight view will be foreshortened by a tall object or bright colours at the far end of it. If, on the other hand, the distant end has a scaled-down ornament and misty, pale colours, the ornament will appear to be further away.

A straight lawn can be narrowed towards the further end to make it seem longer, and the effect can be enhanced by using a bright splash of colour near the beginning. If your garden is wide but not very deep, you can give an impression of enhanced depth by positioning a mirror almost opposite the entrance, surrounded by plants. As you step outside, you seem to see an entrance to another hidden part of the garden.

If the area is surrounded by walls, they can be painted white (for extra light), green (to blend in), or with a floral mural where the planting is sparse. Shaped trellises can be added to give the impression of a distant perspective rather than a flat wall, and a false doorway with a *trompe-l'oeil* vista disappearing

away behind it can be wonderfully effective at enlarging a confined space. The key is not to overdo either the effects or the planting. Mix the elements, making sure that the vertical aspect of the garden is catered for as well as the horizontal. Even a small plot can usually support climbers and containers, as well as a tree, as long as it is in proportion with the rest of the garden scheme.

Above: *A cleverly positioned mirror will reflect the plants back into the garden, suggesting it is larger than it actually is.*

Left: *Features such as this arched trellis will create the illusion of distance in a small garden.*

Opposite: *Statuary placed at the bottom of the garden will draw the eye down the garden's length.*

Choosing Plants for the Back Garden

Every plant has a preference about its ideal growing conditions, and putting a plant in the right spot will mean the difference between it thriving or merely surviving. Certain plants prefer to grow in soils that are higher or lower in acidity than others, while some cannot tolerate acidity at all.

KNOW YOUR SOIL

Avoid expensive mistakes by choosing a plant that is suitable for the soil where it is to be grown. The best way to ascertain the soil pH level is to buy a testing kit, because the levels do vary considerably within even local areas, depending on where the topsoil was brought in from, or what the underlying rock is.

The pH of the soil is influenced by the underlying bedrock, the amount of rainfall, the rate of drainage and also nearby vegetation such as pine trees (which produce acid foliage).

SOIL STRUCTURE

The soil in which the plants are to grow is a collection of minerals and organic matter (humus) which will be expected to support the plant throughout its life. To be able to do this, they usually need a little bit of help in the form of organic matter and fertilizer.

Soil consists of sand, silt, clay and humus, and the proportions in which each is present will determine the structure of the soil – its consistency and water-retaining properties. The more large sand particles it contains, the more easily water will drain through it and the more quickly it will warm up in spring, allowing earlier planting. Silt particles are smaller, so water is held for longer, but they retain little in the way of nutrients. Clay particles are smallest of all; they hold on to nutrients and water extremely well, but produce a heavy, solid soil that is cold (slow to warm up in spring, because the water has to warm up as well as the particles), and prone to damage if it is worked when it is too wet.

The ideal soil to have is a loam, which contains a perfect balance of all the elements, producing a crumbly soil, often dark in colour, which holds both moisture and nutrients well, without becoming water-logged. Unfortunately, this is rare, and most gardens have a soil that favours one particle size over the others and so needs help in the form of added organic matter to make it easier to work. This can take the form of well-rotted manure or compost (soil mix). Organic matter adds air to a solid soil and keeps moisture for longer in a free-draining one.

TESTING THE SOIL pH

1 Take a sample of soil from the area to be tested from about 10cm (4in) under the soil surface. To get a representative sample from the whole garden, take at least five small samples from all over the plot. Mix them together thoroughly in a screw-top jar.

2 Thoroughly mix the soil and indicator chemicals, according to the instructions on the pack.

3 Add liquid to the soil/chemical mixture in the container and shake it vigorously.

4 Compare the colour of the liquid to the chart, to find the pH level of the soil.

Left: *A pH meter will enable you to get an accurate reading of the soil's acidity.*

PLANTS FOR ALKALINE SOIL

Acanthus spinosus
Actinidia kolomikta
Astrantia major
Berberis (all)
Caryopteris x clandonensis
Ceanothus (all)
Deutzia (all)
Dianthus (all)
Euonymus (all)
Exochorda x macrantha
 'The Bride'

Hebe (all)
Hibiscus syriacus
Hypericum (all)
Lonicera (all)
Olearia (all)
Paeonia delaveyi
Potentilla fruticosa
Rosmarinus (rosemary; all)
Spiraea japonica
Verbascum chaixii

PLANTS FOR ACID SOIL

Alchemilla mollis
Andromeda polifolia
 'Compacta'
Azalea
Calluna vulgaris cultivars
Camellia japonica
Camellia x williamsii
Cornus kousa var. chinensis
Corylopsis pauciflora
Cryptomeria japonica
Enkianthus capanulatus
Erica cultivars

Hydrangea
Iris germanica
Magnolia stellata
Meconopsis betonicifolia
Pieris japonica
Rhododendron
Rhodohypoxis baurii
Trachelospermum
 jasminoides
Trillium grandiflorum
Tropaeolum speciosum
 (herbaceous nasturtium)

Above: Potentilla fruticosa *favours alkaline soils.*

Above: Acanthus spinosus *needs a cool, moist, alkaline soil.*

Left: Alchemilla mollis *will grow in acid soil and is enjoyed for its silvery foliage and yellow blooms in spring.*

Above: *The easy-to-grow* Tropaeolum speciosum *(herbaceous nasturtium) is a colourful climber.*

Sun or Shade?

In every garden, there will be parts that are sunnier or shadier than others, and this will be influenced by overhanging trees, tall buildings and high walls as much as by the direction in which the garden faces.

WISE DECISIONS

Putting a plant in the wrong place for its growing preferences will cause it to become stressed, slowing down the growth, reducing the flowering and, ultimately, killing it. Garden centres today are filled with plants from all over the world, from the hottest areas to the coolest, so there will definitely be a range of plants for any situation.

The plants that enjoy being in a hot place often hail originally from Mediterranean regions, and have silver or blue leaves to reflect the light. This is one of the many ways in which plants can adapt to live in particular conditions. Other adaptations include having leaves that are rolled or covered with a waxy coating, to reduce the amount of moisture lost through the leaf-pores, or leaves that have been reduced to spines.

Plants growing in shady areas, such as under a canopy of tall trees, evolve large, soft leaves in order to absorb the maximum amount of available light, and they tend to be dark green with chlorophyll, to be as efficient at producing food as possible.

PLANTS FOR SHADY AREAS

Astantia (moist shade)
Astilbe (moist shade)
Aucuba japonica (dry shade)
Camellia (moist shade)
Dicentra spectabilis (moist shade)
Fatsia japonica (moist shade)
Hamamelis mollis (moist shade)
Helleborus (moist shade)
Hosta (moist shade)
Ilex (dry shade)
Mahonia (moist shade)
Pachysandra terminalis (dry shade)
Rhododendron (moist shade)
Rodgersia (moist shade)
Sarcococca (moist shade)
Skimmia (dry shade)
Viburnum davidii (moist shade)

Above: *Ferns enjoy moist shade and will add lush greenery to your garden scheme.*

Opposite: *Most gardens are a combination of sunny and shady areas, although some may be predominantly one or the other. Choose plants accordingly for garden success.*

Above: *The summer-flowering* Hemerocallis *is easy to grow in sun or partial shade.*

Left: Monarda *'Squaw' is enjoyed for its aromatic foliage and flowers. It requires moist soil.*

PLANTS FOR SUNNY AREAS

Agapanthus
Alchillea filipendulina
Caryopteris x *clandonensis*
Cistus
Convolvulus cneorum
Cytisus
Echinops vitro
Pelargonium
Iris germanica hybrids
Helianthemum nummularium
Kniphofia hybrids
Monarda
Santolina chamaecyparissus
Senecio
Verbascum
Yucca

Storage Space

The need to store less attractive bits and pieces – such as the clothes line or dustbin (trash can) – is a fact of life, but the clutter does not have to be on show. With a little imagination, it can be completely disguised behind a colourful, living screen.

MEANS OF DISGUISE

In an ideal world, garbage bins and recycling containers would be beautiful in themselves, but, unfortunately, in reality they are seldom an attractive sight. They are necessary, however, and they do need to be accessible.

You can simply ignore your garbage cans or spend a little time and effort blending them in, by painting them to co-ordinate with the overall scheme (if this is feasible), using a screen of plants to hide them or camouflaging them with a trellis with plants growing up it.

You will need to consider external factors, such as the amount of room available and how the area is to be accessed. Plant screens, in particular, tend to take up quite a lot of space widthways as they age, and they need regular attention to prevent them from becoming straggly.

Above right: *Here, a trellis grown with climbers was erected to obscure the view of the garden shed. The shed was painted to match the trellis to allow it to blend as much as possible into its surroundings.*

Opposite: *Clever use has been made of the area below the verandah, alllowing access to tools without taking up space that could be used for plants.*

ERECTING A TRELLIS

The advantages of using a trellis are that it is compact, long-lasting, and attractive in its own right. Even without a lot of plants, with a coat of paint or varnish to tone with the surrounding colour scheme, a trellis can harmonize with the surroundings. If you then train plants against or over it, you will introduce an extra dimension that will bring colour and interest throughout the year.

1 Dig a hole at least 60cm (2ft) deep, deeper in light soils. Put the post in the prepared hole and partly fill with dry-mix concrete. Check the post with a spirit level (carpenter's level).

2 Continue filling the hole with concrete, ramming it down firmly.

3 The post should now be firm enough to work on, and once the concrete has "cured" it will be permanently safe. Dig the hole for the next post. Nail the panel on to the first post.

4 Place the second post in its hole and nail it to the panel. Fill the second hole with dry-mix concrete, tamping it down as you proceed. Repeat the steps by digging the third post hole, nailing on the second panel, nailing and positioning the third post and so on, until the trellis is complete. This is more accurate than putting in all the posts and then fixing the panels as, inevitably, some gaps will be too large and some too small.

The Surface

Changing the material covering the "floor" of the garden can completely alter its appearance, by changing the perception of length or width, or by giving a definite flow of design, leading the eye onwards into the garden itself.

PRACTICAL CONSIDERATIONS

The "floor" surface in the garden fulfils the same function, in design terms, as a fitted carpet inside the house, providing a unifying link that flows through the area. It is the foil against which the planting can be arranged and, for every group of planting, there should be a balancing amount of open space.

The surface should also be practical. For instance, wooden decking positioned under overhanging trees will quickly become covered with slippery algae. Paving can be natural stone, brick, or concrete, and it can be laid in lines to lengthen the appearance of the garden, or in patterns to shorten it. Decking and timber are both softer than paving, and are very flexible materials to work with, both in terms of actual installation, and in how they are treated (stained or painted) afterwards. Timber can be mixed with other surfaces, such as paving and gravel, to give interesting textural variations, and laying it across, rather than along,

the run of the path will make the distance look shorter. Railway sleepers (ties) are extremely useful in the garden, and can be used for edging borders and making raised beds as well as edging paths.

Small changes in contour and direction will alter the appearance of the garden, and can be used to give an interesting shape and pleasing sense of proportion. Steps should be wide enough to be functional, especially where food is carried, and shallow enough to be safe for both the very young and the not-so-very young.

Above: *A curved path creates visual interest and a greater sense of space. A well-defined edge contains the planted border.*

Left: *A paved patio is broken up by areas of planting. The plants also offer a degree of privacy by screening and separating off the dining area from the rest of the garden.*

Opposite: *A small paved patio area teeming with plant life and pots of different heights.*

LAYING PAVERS

1 Clay pavers look like bricks but are thinner and are designed to fit together without mortar joints. Prepare a sub-base of 5–10cm (2–4in) of compacted hardcore. Mortar into position a firm edge to work from. Lay a 5cm (2in) bed of sand, making sure the pavers are level with the edging. Adjust the depth of the sand if necessary. Use battens (laths) as a height gauge to enable the sand to be levelled with a piece of wood.

2 Lay the pavers in the required pattern, making sure that they butt up to each other and the edging.

3 Tamp the pavers in place using a club hammer over a length of timber. You could also hire a flat-plate vibrator to do the job. Brush more sand over the pavers to fill the joints, then tamp down again to lock in position.

Screening to Provide Privacy

Privacy is important in the garden, particularly around the area intended for eating or relaxation. Plants, used either as a living screen or to clothe an artificial one, are the ideal solution.

REAL SOLUTIONS

It is difficult to relax completely in the garden if there is no sense of privacy and protection from outside interference, or if something can be seen which is better left hidden, such as storage areas or rubbish bins (trash cans). The problem can be physical, visual or psychological, but if it is essential to the enjoyment of the garden, it should be addressed.

You can increase the height of too-low walls and fences by adding a trellis to the top. This will create a barrier to deter nearby animals from trying to enter, without preventing contact with people on the other side or blocking the view completely. Painting the trellis will add interest until the plants have grown to cover it and will help harmonize it with the surroundings.

If the item to be hidden is within the garden and is not too large, such as a compost container or tool shed, a single evergreen shrub or conifer should suffice to hide it from view. If there is one intrusive eyesore beyond the boundary of the garden that is spoiling the

view, a strategically placed upright tree or conifer may be the answer, so that the offending object is hidden but the rest of the scene can still be appreciated.

If taller protection is required, trees such as birch (*Betula pendula*) are excellent for screening from nearby houses. Because the leaf canopy is light and airy it will not block out too much light.

Privacy is particularly desirable around an eating area, and again, a trellis is useful, as it provides screening without blocking out

Top right: *A trellis can blend in well with the surroundings. It should act as a deterrent to animals without blocking out light or the view beyond.*

Right: *Tall hedges provide a dense and very effective screen.*

the light, is durable, supports plants easily and can be painted or stained to suit the area. Its main disadvantage is that it allows in cold winds. Wattle fences, bamboo and reed screens are also extremely attractive, although they are not as long-lasting as trellises. More flexibly, shrubs, tall grasses and small trees in containers can all act as screens, and can be moved to different positions according to need.

For a more solid barrier, especially where a wall cannot be built, a fence of closely spaced boards will provide good shelter. Close-board, interlock and interwoven fencing is usually available in 2m (6ft) wide panels of varying heights.

PLANTS FOR SCREENING

Arundinaria nitida
Buxus sempervirens
Carpinus betulus
Chamaecyparis lawsoniana
  'Green Hedger'
Crataegus monogyna
Elaeagnus x *ebbingei*
Escallonia 'Iveyi'
Fagus sylvatica
Griselinia littoralis
Ilex aquifolium
Ligustrum ovalifolium
Osmanthus delaveyi
Prunus cerasifera
Prunus laurocerasus
Pyracantha 'Mohave'
Taxus baccata
Thuja orientalis
Ulmus parvifolia
Viburnum rhytidophyllum

Right: *A combination of trees and plants of different heights has been used to shield one part of the garden from the next.*

Using Climbers

A screen, whether a trellis or a hedge, will look more interesting throughout the year if other plants are used to liven it up. There is at least one climbing plant in flower during every month of the year and combining these with the screen will add an extra dimension.

ENHANCING SCREENS

Many of the plants that have the best screening qualities, in terms of large, evergreen leaves, are fairly consistent in their appearance all year round. While this means that the screen is highly effective, it can be a little monotonous. To liven it up, climbers can be trained into it, to grow through and be supported by it. The flowers of the climber then peep through, with the plain foliage of the screen acting as a foil to their colour. A large screen can act as host to several climbers, with flowering periods that follow on from each other, so that the screen is colourful for most of the year. If the climber produces interesting seed heads as well as attractive flowers, you have even more scope. Such is the case with *Clematis tangutica,* the seed heads of which persist well into the winter months.

Some climbers are more vigorous than others, so it is important to choose ones that are compatible with the plants forming the screen, otherwise the screen may be swamped or the climbers may be lost. The screen needs to be established and growing well before the climbers are introduced, or it will not be big enough to give the climbers the support they need.

Where the screen is made of timber or plastic, of course, there is no need to wait before plants are placed against it, unless the wood has recently been treated with a wood preservative which could harm them. Place the plants at the base of the screen, about 15cm (6in) out into the border, and use a cane to guide the stems towards the screen. As the stems begin to grow, weave them into the screen until they become established. Against a fence, the stems will need to be held in place with a system of wires and ties, but these will soon be hidden behind the foliage.

CLIMBERS TO GROW THROUGH TREES OR HEDGES

Akebia quinata
Aristolochia macrophylla
Clematis alpina 'Frances Rivis'
Clematis macropetala 'Markham's Pink'
Clematis montana 'Elizabeth'
Clematis tangutica
Codonopsis clematidea
Eccremocarpus scaber
Humulus lupulus 'Aureus'
Ipomoea lobata
Jasminum officinale 'Aureum'
Lathyrus latifolius
Lonicera x *heckrotii*
Passiflora caerulea
Rosa 'Rambling Rector'
Rosa 'Zéphirine Drouhin'
Thunbergia alata
Tropaeolum speciosum
Tropaeolum peregrinum
Vitis 'Brant'

Above: *Climbing roses have been trained over an arch, providing a screen from one part of the garden to the next, and creating an illusion of space.*

Below left: *Bougainvillea is a beautiful climber suited to sunny gardens.*

Below: Clematis *'Perle d'Azur' provides a gorgeous splash of colour in the garden.*

PLANTING A CLIMBER

1 Dig a hole large enough to accommodate the rootball of the plant, and fork plenty of well-rotted compost or manure into the base.

2 Check the depth of the hole (the level in the container should be slightly below the final soil level) and then remove the container and place the rootball in the hole.

3 Refill the hole with topsoil and a small amount of fertilizer, firm it down and water the area well.

4 Position a cane close to the base of the climbing plant and use it to guide the stems of the climber towards the host plant.

Above: Vinca major *has been planted to grow up through a hedge, providing additional colour to a practical screening solution.*

Lighting

There is no reason why you can't enjoy your garden even after darkness has fallen. Lighting can be used to give a completely different appearance to plants and features such as water or statuary. Using lighting in the garden at night expands the usable living area and creates a mood, as well as having purely practical effects, such as discouraging intruders, or showing up changes of level and other hazards. It allows the best features to be highlighted while leaving others hidden, and brings the garden to life in a totally different way.

USING ELECTRICITY

Electric lighting can be used among the plants in different directions. "Up-lighting" entails positioning light fixtures so the object is lit from below, making a dramatic focal glow in the garden. It is extremely effective for highlighting coloured leaves in the autumn, a tree with interesting bark, or a statue. When "down-lighting", the object or area is lit from above, for safety or security reasons, or to give a softer, more diffuse overall light. Done well, it can imitate natural light – moonlight gently passing through trees, for instance.

Above: *A lantern is suspended from the same bracket as a hanging basket. The soft light will enhance the flowers after sunset.*

Left: *A candle display cleverly designed to emphasize garden paraphernalia: candles in vegetable shapes share storage space with terracotta pots.*

If you have more than one circuit installed you will have more flexibility. Lights can be switched on and off at different times to create different effects.

CANDLES AND LANTERNS

Lighting does not have to involve electricity, however; in its simplest form, it need be no more than candles, flares or lanterns. Candles may not provide much light but they are wonderful for atmosphere, and outdoor ones often deter insects, too. Flares resemble large candles, burn for 6–8 hours, and cast a warm, romantic glow. Lanterns, either candle or oil, can be hung or stood around the garden to cast a gentle, golden light.

Whatever system of lighting you choose, use it to enhance the garden and seating area subtly, rather than flooding them with a great glare of light. Garden lighting will need to be totally waterproof if it is to be left outside permanently and, if it is to be used in water, it will need to be approved waterproof underwater lighting. Candles, flares and lanterns should never be left unattended, and should be kept out of the reach of children and animals.

Right: *This light hidden among ivy draws attention to the lush greenery as well as lighting the boundaries of the garden path.*

The Courtyard and Patio

Tiny as these areas may be in the city, the courtyard and patio can become the "room outside", where eating is a relaxed and social experience, surrounded by foliage, flowers and fragrances.

The term "patio" originally referred to an inner courtyard set among the living rooms of a building. Nowadays, it refers to almost any hard-surface area in the garden, although usually the one where the outdoor furniture is sited.

While the patio is often placed adjacent to the house, this is not critical. You may find it is better positioned to make the most of the evening sunlight. If this is at the bottom of the garden, make sure the access routes are planned properly.

Privacy and a feeling of seclusion are important to help make the area a relaxing one in which to sit, and some form of screening may play a part in creating this. The whole area should be designed to have a harmonious feel, with the colours of the furniture, accessories and plants all chosen to complement each other.

Opposite: *This patio area uses pots to shield the house and paving from the rest of the garden.*

Patio Surfaces

As with the rest of the garden, the surface sets the mood in the courtyard or on the patio. It should be in keeping with the surroundings and practical for the situation.

PAVING

There are many different types of paving available, in a range of materials, shapes and sizes. Traditional Yorkstone paving is attractive and hard-wearing, but is expensive. There are many concrete imitations that are equally attractive, widely available and much cheaper. Larger paving slabs can be smooth or textured ("riven"), and their use will depend on the purpose of the patio. Young children might find some of the textured slabs difficult to walk or ride a small bicycle across, and furniture placed on them may be slightly unsteady. In order to create a variety of patterns, the slabs can be square, rectangular or hexagonal, and they are designed to be easily laid on to a level, well-prepared base. Small paving blocks (paviours) and house bricks are equally easy to lay, although this does take a little longer because you have to lay so many more of them. They can be laid in a number of decorative patterns, such as basket-weave and herringbone; or used to change the apparent perspective of the area. By laying them crossways you will shorten the view, whereas lengthways they will extend it.

Right: A small seating area with chair postioned to catch the most of the sun.

LAYING PAVING

1 Lay a bed of hardcore, roughly 15cm (6in) deep and rake it roughly level.

2 Make five small mounds ("spots") of mortar, one to fit under each corner of the slab, and one for the centre. Lower the slab into a horizontal position on the sand spots.

3 Gently wiggle the slab from side to side, to bed it down on to the mortar spots, and check that it is level by placing a spirit level (carpenter's level) diagonally across it to get an accurate reading.

4 Repeat across the opposite diagonal. Repeat the whole process with the remaining slabs, placing each alongside the previous one and aligning with an even gap along the joint.

Above: *Paving stones come in a wide variety of textures and colours to suit every taste and budget.*

continued...

WOODEN DECKING

Using wood as a surface has always been popular in countries with a plentiful supply of timber, but it is becoming more and more popular elsewhere as a result of its sheer flexibility. Decking can be used in the smallest of areas, is light to handle, easy to lay, and can be cut to fit even the most awkward shape with ease. It will cope with uneven surfaces that would be difficult and expensive to level and, unlike hard surfaces such as concrete, it can be laid around an established plant or tree without causing any damage. The open nature of the decking means that the plant will still receive rainfall around its roots and continue to grow undisturbed, although some allowance for the expansion of the trunk will have to be made when the timber is measured to fit.

The colour of the wood for the decking can be chosen to complement the surroundings, either by staining or painting. Soft greys, greens and blues all make a perfect foil for nearby plants. This effect can be enhanced by using the same colours to stain any nearby trellis, wooden furniture or containers.

Timber for decking can be of hard- or softwood, but it must be properly treated to ensure its durability. Hardwood should then need only periodic brushing with a stiff brush and some fungicide; softwoods will need an annual treatment with a wood preservative (one that will not harm plants).

Above: *Decking provides a durable, practical and easy-to-care-for floor surface for the patio or courtyard.*

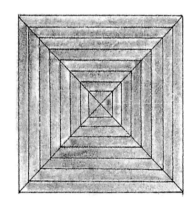
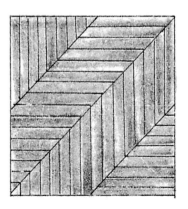
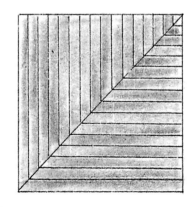

Left: *Wooden decking can be laid in a number of decorative patterns.*

The Seating Area

Create a relaxed area in which to sit and enjoy a mild spring day or a warm summer evening undisturbed. When thinking of the garden in terms of a "room outside", it is important to include a seating area where it can be enjoyed to the full. There is no need to think in grand terms: a simple rustic chair is sufficient in a small garden, and will provide an excuse to rest and unwind amid the sights and sounds of nature.

DESIGN PRACTICALITIES

The scale of the area allocated to seating should reflect its intended use, and may be much larger in a warm area than a cold one where conditions do not favour lingering outdoors. Ideally, the furniture should be situated in a position to enjoy sunshine at the time of day it will be used, even if this is not an area adjacent to the house. It can always be linked to the house for the purposes of carrying food and drinks safely, by a specially created and planted walkway.

The planting around the seating area should provide privacy and shelter, shielding it from intrusions by the outside world. It can also be used to give shade if the area is a hot one. Climbers such as jasmine, honeysuckle, wisteria and rose will provide shade, and their flowers will fill the air with perfume on warm evenings.

Introduce additional plants, either permanently or on a seasonal basis, by using containers. Place them at the entrance to the area, massed to one side, or use them to

brighten a dark corner. Containers can be colour-coordinated with the furniture, chosen to look like part of the garden in natural, earthy shades or hidden altogether under a mass of lush, trailing foliage.

Extend the use of the seating area and create a wonderful atmosphere by installing lighting, from simple oil lamps or candles to a more complex electrical system. Your enjoyment of the garden will not then be restricted to daylight hours, and the lighting will endow the plants with a completely new look.

Left: *Here, a trellis frames the seating area. Lanterns provide candlelight in the evenings while the structure itself is painted to complement adjacent plants.*

Above: *This tiny patio area adjacent to the house catches plenty of sun. Tubs, planters and a window box soften the bricks and paving.*

Plants in Paving

Whether the paving is a path or a patio, it will look much less stark, especially when it is new, if a few small, low-growing plants are added in among the slabs to soften and blur the edges.

SOFTENING EDGES

There is no reason why a paved area has to be a barren, plantless desert, unless it is by choice. By taking up the occasional paving slab or brick, or by scraping back the gravel, it is possible to add small plants that will grow only slowly and withstand being stepped on occasionally. Such plants work well to blend the hard surface into the garden, by integrating the two. This is especially desirable when the paving is new and clean, with sharp, well-defined edges. Long before the slabs begin to look weathered, the plants will have grown to give a much softer appearance to the area. Low-growing thymes are extremely effective at this, because, if they are walked on, the damaged leaves release oils that evaporate to give off their distinctive fragrance. For purely practical purposes, it may be useful to plant an ant-repellent such as pennyroyal *(Mentha pulegium)* near to a doorway if ants are known to be a problem, rather than use a chemical.

As with any other planting scheme, the plants should be chosen to match the situation as closely as possible, with the sun-lovers in the hot areas, and the moisture-lovers in shadier parts.

1 Chisel out a few planting crevices if the paving is cemented, or clear out some of the old soil. Remove to a depth of at least 5cm (2in).

2 Fill the holes with a loam-based compost (soil mix) leaving space to plant.

3 Use small plants, seedlings or recently rooted cuttings. Tease away most of the soil to make insertion easier. Trickle more compost around the roots after planting. Firm gently and remove pockets of air.

4 Water carefully. A fine mist from a compression sprayer is less likely to wash away soil than a watering can. Water regularly but avoid a forceful jet of water until the plants are established.

Above: *The spring-flowering* Aubrieta *is a popular choice for planting among paving and edging paths.*

Opposite: *Grow plants in the spaces between pavings, as here, or remove entire slabs for a larger display of plants.*

PLANTS TO GROW IN PAVING

Ajuga reptans 'Burgundy Glow'
Alchemilla mollis
Armeria maritima
Aubrieta cultivars
Campanula portenschlagiana
Chamaemelum nobile
Dianthus deltoides
Lysimachia nummularia
Pulmonaria angustifolia
Liriope muscari

Mentha requienii
Saponaria ocymoides
Saxifraga moschata
Sedum acre 'Aureum'
Sedum spurium 'Schorbuser Blut'
Sempervivum tectorum
Thymus herba-barona
Thymus vulgaris 'Silver Posie'
Vinca minor
Viola species

Garden Furniture

There is an enormous choice of furniture available for the garden, from folding plastic chairs, which can be stored in a shed until they are required, to whole suites of hardwood dining furniture.

CARING FOR FURNITURE AND ACCESSORIES

For seating that is to be left outside all year, it is as well to choose a durable material such as teak or painted metal, which will need only annual maintenance. Softer woods should always be well seasoned and treated with preservative, and this will need renewing at least once a year. Plastic needs little maintenance apart from a good wash, but has a limited life outdoors and will eventually become brittle. To harmonize the accessories with the garden, a number of acrylic paints are available that can be applied to wood, metal and terracotta to make them look less glaringly new. A shiny galvanized bucket can be given the verdigris effect of ageing copper by applying a coat of primer, a base coat of

dark grey-green, and then shades of green in a stippled pattern.

The walls surrounding the garden or seating area can also be transformed by painting them in complementary colours. A dark garden can be lightened by reflecting the available light off white- or (less glaringly) cream-painted walls. Using a muted, soft green will blur the wall into the planting, making the boundary less distinct and the garden seem bigger. On a more bold note, bright sunshine yellows and rich blues will liven up a dull area or a small courtyard and provide a splash of colour behind strong, lush foliage.

DISTRESSING WOODEN FOLDING CHAIRS

Folding chairs are readily available and will weather with age. They can be enhanced with this simple effect.

1 Rub down the surface of the chair with sandpaper to provide a better surface for the paint to adhere to. Rub over the surface randomly with a household candle, applying the wax thickly on the corners and the edges.

2 Paint the chair with white emulsion (latex) paint using random brush strokes and leave to dry completely. Rub down the paintwork with wire (steel) wool to remove the paint from the waxed areas.

Above: *Give a new, plain wooden chair a distressed look.*

Far left: *Metal furniture is robust enough to need very little maintenance over the winter.*

Opposite: *Wicker furniture can be left natural or painted if it is no longer looking its best.*

Planting for Height

Planting for the "third dimension", height, really allows all the space within the patio or courtyard to be used to the full, and the added heat retained by a south- or west-facing wall will protect more tender and exotic plants.

PLANTING IDEAS

Having a wall to plant against adds a whole extra dimension to your possibilities, especially if it faces south or west, because the heat from the sun is absorbed during the day and given off overnight. Nearby plants will be kept several degrees warmer than those beyond the wall's influence. This allows the planting of subjects that could not survive without the extra heat.

Most shrubs can be grown near a wall. Wall-shrubs are specifically those that can be pruned back to form a covering for the wall, supported against it using wires and ties, and through which other plants such as climbers can be grown. Climbers support themselves in a number of ways: by twining their stems around a support; by twisting tendrils or leaf-stalks around a support; by using thorns to scramble; or by the use of aerial roots or sucker pads to attach themselves.

Whether the plant is intended for a wall or a pergola, it should be of a size chosen to be in context with its surroundings, otherwise it will need regular pruning to keep it under control, and this may be at the expense of the flowers. Do bear in mind that, after rainfall, the plant will drip for some time, and this may result in the surface underneath becoming slippery. If this is also a well-used route through the garden, it may be advisable to replace a smooth surface, such as decking, with a non-slip one, such as gravel. This can be edged with brick or bonded with resin to keep it from interfering with mowing the lawn.

PLANTS FOR WALLS

Actinidia kolomikta
Ampelopsis brevipedunculata
Arbutus unedo
Campsis x *tagliabuana*
  'Madame Galen'
Carpenteria californica
Chaenomeles speciosa
  'Moerloosei'
Clematis armandii
  'Apple Blossom'
Crinodendron hookerianum
Eucryphia x *nymansensis*
'Nymansay'
Fremontodendron

'California Glory'
Garrya elliptica 'James Roof'
Hedera colchica
  'Sulphur Hear'
Hedera helix 'Buttercup'
Itea ilicifolia
Jasminum nudiflorum
Magnolia grandiflora
Parthenocissus tricuspidata
  'Veitchii'
Rosa 'Mermaid'
Trachelospermum
  jasminoides
Vitis coignetiae

ATTACHING A TRELLIS TO A WALL

1 Take the trellis to the wall and mark its position. Drill holes for fixing spacers and insert plastic or wooden plugs.

2 Drill the equivalent holes in the wooden batten and secure it to the wall, checking with a spirit level that it is horizontal. Use a piece of wood that holds the trellis at least 2.5 cm (1 in) from the wall. Fix a similar batten at the base and one half-way up for a trellis above 1.2 m (4 ft) high.

3 Drill and screw the trellis to the battens, first fixing the top and then working downwards. Check that the trellis is not crooked.

4 The finished trellis should be fixed tightly to the wall so that the weight of the climber or any wind that blows on it will not pull it away from its fixings.

Opposite: *Make the most of available space by planting climbers up a trellis.*

continued...

PLANTS FOR PERGOLAS

Akebia quinata
Campsis radicans
Clematis 'Bill MacKenzie'
Clematis campaniflora
Clematis rehderiana
Clematis viticella
Humulus lupulus 'Aureus'
Jasminum x *stephanense*
Laburnum x *watereri* 'Vossii'
Lathyrus latifolius
Lonicera x *brownii*
  'Dropmore Scarlet'
Lonicera japonica 'Halliana'
Lonicera x *tellmanniana*
Parthenocissus henryana
Passiflora caerulea
Rosa 'Zéphirine Drouhin'
Solanum jasminoides 'Album'
Thunbergia alata
Wisteria floribunda
Wisteria sinensis

GROWING CLIMBERS ON WIRES

Above: *Growing climbers will allow you to make the most of the space in your garden.*

1 For walls, wedge-shaped vine eyes can be hammered in place. Those with screw-fixings can be used on walls or wooden fences or posts, first drilling and plugging holes.

2 Thread galvanized wire through the hole in the vine eye and wrap it round itself. Thread through the intermediate eyes (at no more than 180cm (6ft) intervals). Fasten off the wire firmly.

3 Curve long stems over the wires, using either plastic ties or string. Tie at several points if necessary. Tie the stems in a series of arches, rather than straight up, to encourage flowering buds.

Growing Herbs

Herbs are ideal plants for the patio or courtyard. The sheltered aspect allows plants suited to Mediterranean climates to thrive, and they can be grown in small pots or boxes, taking up little space and providing fresh flavours for cooking throughout the summer.

HERBAL BENEFITS

The use of herbs for medicinal and culinary purposes dates back to the dawn of civilization, when basic trial and error proved that certain plants were useful, while others were downright dangerous. Care must always be taken in the use of plants if they are to be ingested, but they are an invaluable addition to the garden.

Herbs are a particularly good choice for the area close to the house, such as a patio or courtyard, for a number of reasons. Most herbs are used in the kitchen during cooking, so it makes sense to have them close by for easy collection, even in the rain. Placing herbs near the house also means that their wonderful fragrance can be appreciated to the full as it wafts in through the open windows, so the patio or courtyard is the ideal place.

Many of the most popular herbs have their origins in the countries of the Mediterranean region, and need a warm, dry position in which to flourish. If the garden does not have these conditions, the answer is to grow them in containers, handily placed near the kitchen door, where the drainage is good and they can be moved around to make the most of the available light. Herbs are a boon for the area where you plan to be sitting and eating al fresco, because some of them have excellent properties as insect repellants: pennyroyal *(Mentha pulegium)* keeps ants away, basil discourages flies and scented plants such as lavender and rosemary deter mosquitoes.

Left: *Rosemary may be grown in pots or as an informal hedge. There are cultivars available with flowers in various shades of blue, white and pink.*

Right: *Even in the tiniest spaces you can plant up a wooden box with a selection of different herbs, providing ample variety for cooking throughout the summer months.*

PLANTING UP A HERB BOX

1 Cover the base of a wooden box with a layer of broken pots or coarse gravel to improve drainage, followed by a covering of compost (soil mix).

2 Arrange the herb plants inside the trough and place a small amount of compost around the base of each plant, to hold them in position.

3 Fill the trough with compost until it is level with the rim. Firm it gently around the plants. Water the trough, to settle the compost and remove any air-pockets around the plants' roots. Cover the surface of the compost with a layer of coarse gravel to act as a mulch.

Using Containers

Using pots, troughs and urns on the patio or in the courtyard will soften hard edges, extend the growing area and can create spectacular focal points. Displays of containers are an attractive and varied means of harmonizing the soft landscaping of the garden with the hard surfaces of the patio or courtyard.

ADAPTABLE DISPLAYS

Containers come in an enormous range of shapes, sizes and colours, and in a variety of different materials. In addition, they can be chosen or easily customized with a paint effect to match other accessories within the garden.

Introducing containers into a town garden means that all of the available space can be used to the full; it also allows the creation of movable displays in a way that is simply not possible in the garden itself. Plants can be grown in the most inhospitable places without relying on the local growing environment.

Arrangements can be changed seasonally, moved around to provide an instant display in a particular area or simply placed to make the most of the available light. You have more flexibility in the choice of plants destined for a container, enabling you to grow those with a definite soil pH preference (such as rhododendrons or camellias), or those that prefer a dry site, in areas where the natural soil would not be suitable.

It is important to view plants in containers as integral parts of the garden, rather than as separate entities, and use them to extend the growing area into the hard-surface area. To this end, the plants chosen should include a mixture of both foliage and flowering varieties, so that the arrangement has structure as well as colour.

Position the pots around the entrance way or to edge stairs and paths to link the garden with the inside of the house.

PLANTS FOR CONTAINERS

Acer palmatum dissectum
Argyranthemum cultivars
Begonia x *tuberhybrida*
 cultivars
Camellia x *williamsii*
Canna 'Wyoming'
x *Citrofortunella microcarpa*
Cordyline australis
Fuchsia 'Thalia'
Geranium sanguineum
Hosta sieboldiana
 var. *elegans*

Impatiens
 New Guinea hybrids
Laurus nobilis
Lilium 'Casa Blanca'
Magnolia stellata
Osteospermum 'Whirligig'
Rhododendron
 yakushimanum
Sempervivum (houseleeks)
Wisteria (trained as a standard)
Yucca filamentosa 'Variegata'
Zantedeschia aethiopica

PLANTING A CONTAINER

1 Cover the base of the container with a layer of coarse gravel or polystyrene, to help the drainage.

2 Cover the drainage material with a layer of compost (soil mix) until the container is about half full.

3 Arrange the plant(s) inside the container and place compost around each to hold in position. Add compost to the container until it is level with the rim, then firm it around the plant(s).

4 Water the container and remove any air-pockets around the plants' roots. Cover the surface of the compost with a layer of coarse grit, to act as a mulch.

Left: *Container-grown plants can be enhanced by the choice of pot used. Remember this is not a low-maintenance option as the plants will not be able to draw as much nourishment or water from the surrounding soil.*

Opposite: *Arrangements of pots will enable you to grow plants with specific soil requirements, and the combinations can be varied as required.*

Choosing Containers

The vast range of containers available means that they can be chosen to match the situation and the budget. Most containers can be customized and can do a great deal to improve the most unpromising environments.

TYPES OF CONTAINER

There are a multitude of containers on the market, made from a wide range of materials, and of varying quality and durability. One of the oldest is terracotta, either glazed or unglazed, which produces a rough, earthy container; terracotta will blend well in most gardens but looks particularly attractive in a warm, Mediterranean-type setting. It is reasonably durable, as long as it was guaranteed frost-proof when it was bought, otherwise it may shatter during a cold winter. Terracotta is used for pots, strawberry tubs, troughs and wall pots.

Wooden containers, such as half-barrels, tubs and troughs, have a rural look, are natural insulators (keeping plant roots warmer than stone or plastic) and are ideal for an informal setting. Those square wooden planters often called "Versailles", however, can be used very successfully in formal gardens and are particularly effective with very architectural plants,

such as topiary, used in pairs to frame an entrance. How durable wooden containers are will depend upon how well they have been treated and seasoned, and they will probably need continued care as time goes on.

Reconstituted stone is used for larger pots, urns and troughs, and is much heavier than terracotta or wood. For this reason, it is a good choice where the container is likely to be left in position for a long time. These containers are usually highly ornamental, and suit a formal position near the house, at the end of a vista, or at the entrance to a seating area or walkway.

Concrete pots, urns and troughs are similar to reconstituted stone ones, and are equally heavy. Both concrete and reconstituted stone pots should be allowed to weather for several months before lime-hating plants are planted into them.

Plastic pots come in a wide variety of shapes, sizes and

colours, are cheap and light to handle, and unlike the other materials, are not porous, so that water is not lost through the sides. Improvements are constantly being made to increase the durability, but they are still likely to become brittle and crack if they are kept in strong sunlight.

Top: *Baskets can be made of traditional material or of wire.*

Above: *Galvanized tin is used for beautiful planters.*

Left: *Terracotta pots are available in all styles and sizes.*

Opposite: *A wheelbarrow was given a distressed paint effect, then filled with wooden trug baskets and terracotta pots.*

COMPOST (SOIL MIX) FOR CONTAINERS

The two main types of compost (soil mix) available for use in containers are soilless and soil-based. Soilless composts are based on peat, or a peat-substitute such as coir fibre, and are light and easy to handle. They contain sufficient nutrients for at least one growing season, and are suitable for plants that will only be in the container for a maximum of 12 months before being repotted or discarded. They are free-draining and, once they dry out, they can be very difficult to re-wet.

Soil-based composts contain a lot of natural soil, so they are heavier to handle but much better at hanging on to both water and nutrients. Larger or older plants, or those which are to remain in the same pots for a long period of time, will benefit from the stability offered by this type.

THE BALCONY AND ROOF TERRACE

Of all the places to create a garden, a balcony or roof-top must be among the most challenging, especially if the site is exposed. However, the reward of a green haven high above the rest of the world and its bustle is incentive enough to try, and it is much more relaxing to look out on to plants than on to bricks and concrete.

Trailing and climbing plants, lush foliage and bright flowers can all be brought into action to transform a plain, hard area into a delightful secret world, often invisible to those walking below.

This 'room outside' can become a peaceful retreat or a place for entertaining, gently clothed in relaxing shades of green, or it can contain a riot of bright colour. Bare walls can be softened and camouflaged with planting, low walls given height with trellis and plain floors covered by decking. Strategically placed plants can hide intrusive eyesores or windows which overlook the area, to enhance the feeling of privacy.

Opposite: *This terrace serves as an extension to the indoor living space and can be used for entertaining or simply relaxing.*

Exposure to Wind

Gusting wind and turbulence can be difficult for plants and people, but a well-placed windbreak can be disguised behind more tolerant plants, to shelter and protect delicate species planted around the seating area.

CREATING WINDBREAKS

In built-up areas, the wind can really whistle between the "man-made canyons" of tall buildings, causing turbulence and destruction. Poorly fixed containers, light plants and furniture are all at risk of being dislodged or blown down. Plants with soft, tender foliage are likely to be scorched by the wind, resulting in brown, withered leaves and poor growth.

Creating a windbreak will help minimize the problem; one which is partly permeable to the wind is much more effective than a solid one, where localized turbulence is created as the wind hits it and is deflected. Black windbreak netting becomes almost invisible if it is erected and then hidden behind a painted trellis, especially if plants are then grown up the trellis. This form of windbreak is both effective, and does not take up much room – an important consideration when space is at a premium. Where slightly more room is available, a screen of tall, wind-tolerant shrubs installed along the most vulnerable side will act to shelter the area behind them; many plants will tolerate this kind of exposure while still providing colour and interest throughout the year. Using a broken windbreak rather than a solid one also allows full advantage to be taken of the view, so that even a windy day will not spoil the enjoyment of sitting out on the terrace.

WIND-TOLERANT PLANTS

Cornus alba 'Aurea'
Cotinus coggygria
Cryptomeria japonica
Euonymus fortunei cultivars
Gaultheria mucronata
Hamamelis virginiana
Hippophae rhamnoides
Hydrangea paniculata 'Grandiflora'
Kalmia latifolia
Lavatera olbia
Leucothoe walteri
Lonicera pileata
Mahonia aquifolium
Pachysandra terminalis
Philadelphus 'Belle Etoile'
Salix hastata 'Wehrhahnii'
Spiraea japonica
Tamarix tetrandra
Taxus baccata
Thuja occidentalis

ERECTING A WINDBREAK

• If required, paint the posts intended to support the netting and trellis. Attach securely to the railings or wall, with clamps or bolts.

• Attach black windbreak netting to the back of the posts.

• Fix trellis panels to the posts, in front of the netting.

• Train climbing plants to cover the trellis.

Above: Lavatera *is a good choice for windy areas as it is strong and has an abundance of flowers in summer.*

Above: Euonymus *will grow in many unfavourable conditions and can be grown to screen more delicate plants.*

Above: *Bamboo panels act as a windbreak, while a parasol provides protection from the glare of the sun.*

Opposite: *Here, strong fabric acts as a shield for plants while still allowing some light to penentrate.*

Overhead Screening

Used to make the area more secluded or simply to provide shade, overhead screening adds to the atmosphere of the balcony or roof garden by giving it more continuity with the living space inside.

ADAPTABLE SCREENING

Make sure the screening won't make rooms too dark. If this is likely to be a problem, a compromise in the form of a deciduous climber growing over a pergola may be the answer, providing cover during the summer but not the winter, when the light levels are lower.

Pergolas need to be sturdy to support the weight of the covering, but they are extremely versatile. The plants you grow up the sides can range from annuals like sweet peas to woody perennials such as grape vines, always bearing in mind the dimensions of the pergola. The sides can support cane or bamboo screens, if extra privacy is needed, and, if you don't want to grow plants over the top, you can pull over a canvas cover.

Pergolas can be made from anything from the usual rough timber to sleek bamboo poles. You need to choose carefully for the roof garden or balcony, according to how much extra weight can be introduced. Also consider the prevailing wind direction, which might cause a

problem to a high structure if you don't give it extra protection.

Canvas awnings are convenient to install, and can be designed to retract into a casing on the wall when not required. Unbleached sailcloth and lightweight muslin are natural-looking fabrics that will blend with most colour-schemes.

UMBRELLAS AND PARASOLS

Large, off-white canvas umbrellas are ideal for short-term cover where space allows, as long as the wind is not likely to gust and sweep them away.

Patio parasols are available in many colours so you can co-ordinate them with other fabrics. They will need to be anchored through the table into a base.

Above and opposite: *Parasols are an easy form of overhead screening, but may be less suitable for windy sites.*

Left: *A retractable canvas awning is a great solution for overhead screening, as it provides total shelter when required, but can be pulled back when no longer needed.*

Weight on the Balcony

Balconies vary considerably in their construction and appearance, ranging from older, wrought-iron types to functional, modern brick ones. Roofs might not vary so much, but, especially if you are gardening on a flat-roofed extension, you do still need to be sure it is safe.

BUILDING STRUCTURE

Before you begin designing the garden, check the balcony or roof structurally, to make sure that it will bear the additional weight of the plants and containers you intend to bring in. A medium-sized tub, when planted up and watered, can weigh as much as 9kg (20lb), and you are likely to want a good many more than one. This is more likely to be a problem on an older building, where the wear and tear of the years may be taking their toll on the brickwork and mortar. The extra weight is difficult to judge, because it will not be constant, as the containers will weigh more when they have just been watered than as they dry out. This means that they may weigh more in winter than in summer, although this will also depend on local conditions and whether the

plants have shed their leaves or not.

Consider the weight problem at the planning stage. How much extra load your roof or balcony can bear will depend on its construction and age; it is a wise precaution to explain the plans to a qualified builder or architect, and be guided by their opinion. Careful consideration of the materials to be used, however, can keep the extra weight to a minimum. Timber decking or tiles are lighter alternatives to paving slabs and require less effort to handle – a definite advantage for a roof garden, where everything has to be brought up from ground level. Screens of wattle, bamboo and plastic are lighter than timber fencing. Wooden trellis comes in a variety of weights, all of which are heavier than plastic.

Containers themselves also vary considerably in weight; plastic and wood weigh much less than reconstituted stone or concrete, or even terracotta. Even the compost (soil mix) can make a difference, because soil-based composts weigh a great deal more than soilless ones, even when these are wet. The addition of perlite or vermiculite to the compost reduces the weight still

further, although it will also speed up drainage, so you may have to water more often. (Mixing water-retaining gel into the planting mixture when you plant up the containers helps it to retain water.) Every little helps: consider using broken polystyrene in the base of the container, rather than the traditional pieces of broken crockery.

Above: *Polystyrene (plastic foam) is a light option for drainage material. Place at the bottom of the pot before planting.*

Above: *An open-weave wire hanging basket is a better option than stone or terracotta.*

Above: *Baskets can be lined with moss or cardboard, as here. A cardboard liner will absorb less water than a moss one.*

Above: *Plastic is lighter than terracotta. Here, a plastic saucer is placed in the base of a fruit-picking basket (also lightweight). Plants in plastic pots can then be arranged in the basket, and the pots will be disguised.*

Opposite: *If your balcony or terrace is relatively sheltered you can use lightweight material such as cane for furniture and screens.*

Watering and Drainage

Natural rainfall is not always sufficient for plants, even when they are growing in the garden, so it is particularly important to their health that watering is not neglected when they are growing in containers.

WATERING SYSTEMS

In their natural surroundings, many plants survive during periods of low rainfall by extending their roots deep into the earth in search of residual moisture. In containers, they are totally dependent on a regular supply of water to keep them alive.

You can cut down on the need to water frequently by adding water-retaining gel to the compost. This swells up as it absorbs water, and releases it back to the plants as they need it.

Irrigation systems that connect the water supply directly to the plants are an excellent way of cutting down on wasted water, because all the water is delivered exactly where it is needed, at the plants' roots. These can be operated by timing devices to suit the needs of the plants.

As well as providing enough water for your plants, you also need to consider how to get rid of rainwater. On a balcony, excess water can usually be drained away without a problem, but on a roof it may be more difficult. The surplus must drain off quickly, or the roof might not be able to bear the weight.

If you are laying flooring, such as timber decking, it must not interfere with the waterproof membrane covering the roof, and it is important that no damage occurs during installation that would cause water to seep into the rooms below. You should also ensure that canopies will not trap water during bad weather.

Above: *A drip-feed system is ideal for hanging baskets and window boxes. Watering will probably have to be programmed to operate a couple of times a day in hot weather.*

Above: *Drip-feed systems can be used for plants in containers. Use a T-joint to run branches or tubes for individual drip feeds. Even in wet weather, containers under the "rain shadow" of a wall often need additional water.*

Left: *Use spaghetti-feed heads for watering containers. The special pegs will enable you to fix the tube in a suitable position.*

Above: *A timing device will turn your watering system on and off automatically, yet can easily be de-activated if the weather is wet.*

Opposite: *When installing the surface of the terrace make sure it does not interfere with the underlying structure of the roof.*

Access to the Balcony or Roof Terrace

Access routes to the balcony or roof garden are usually pretty straightforward and should not present as many problems as in front gardens, for instance. There are some special considerations for these areas, however. The most important point, which must be borne in mind at the initial planning stage, is that fire escapes need to kept clear – especially when these are shared by neighbours.

KEEP EXITS CLEAR

In an older property, where several flats are reached by means of a system of metal stairs and balconies, the whole appearance of the building can be altered and enhanced by allowing a tracery of climbing plants to grow along the metalwork. The building develops a character all its own and each individual balcony can then become a small garden for its owner, all different, but linked by the overall greenery. However, if the area in which the garden is being created constitutes part of a fire escape, it is essential for safety to keep it clear so people can descend quickly and easily in an emergency. This is particularly important for a communal balcony, where the same escape route is allocated to several flats – the last thing frightened people need in an emergency is to be falling over pots and trellises.

Top right: *Ensure easy access by keeping the area around the door clear of pots and other items.*

Right: *These pots, positioned outside the handrailings on a flight of stairs, are a clever compromise between practicality and decoration as they do not impede access.*

Left: *Climbing plants soften the metal stairs and handrails.*

Safety on the Balcony or Roof Terrace

Safety considerations, such as checking the area has adequate structural strength for the added weight, should be taken care of before you plan your designs. After this, the main necessity is to carry out regular maintenance.

WEATHER

The weather is always an unpredictable element in any equation, simply because it is so variable, even within small, local areas. The funnelling effect of tall buildings may result in strong gusts of wind hitting one balcony while barely affecting another nearby, for instance. The following are the major factors to take into account.

All the fixtures and fittings on the balcony or roof will need to be secured against the possibility of a gust of wind knocking them over or off the edge. Many of the fittings, such as light furniture, can be taken indoors during the worst months of the year. Check permanent features like trellis screens, which will be expected to bear the brunt of the weather, to ensure that they are firmly fixed into position.

Bright sunlight will make plastic brittle after a few years, so plant supports such as trellises made out of this material may break away from the wall.

Excess water can usually be swept off a balcony, but on a roof, getting rid of the water depends on a good drainage system. You should install this first, before bringing in any structures, furniture, containers or plants, to prevent a build-up of water from causing damage to the structure.

Awnings and canopies made of fabric, especially those of natural fibres, are at least twice as heavy when they are wet as when they are dry. If they are stretched across a frame, they can trap large pools of water on top, which may result in the material ripping away from its fixing points, deluging whatever is underneath.

OVERHANGING THE STREET

Where the balcony directly overhangs the street, containers attached to railings must be firmly fixed. Likewise, position any pots on low walls around the edge of the roof garden where they will not cause damage if they happen to over-balance.

Above left: *A small balcony will not need much maintenance. Fabric covered furniture should not be left outside during the winter months, and all fixtures should be checked regularly to make sure they have not come loose.*

Above: *A profusion of windowboxes and pots adorning balconies are a delight to all who pass by. Make sure they are firmly fixed, with brackets if necessary, to ensure they are safe.*

Plant Interest the Year Round

No garden need ever have a time when it looks dull or uninteresting, particularly a roof or balcony garden, which might well be visible all the time just outside the sitting room windows.

PLANTS THAT EARN THEIR KEEP

In any garden, a plant should earn its place, and this is never more important than where space is limited. One season of interest is acceptable if it is spectacular, but two are better and, if a particular plant has pretty flowers in spring or summer and then a wonderful blaze of autumn colour, it has definitely earned its keep.

Of course, not all plants do this; for foliage plants, which act as a foil to more dramatic flowering specimens, it is sufficient that they look gloriously lush throughout the season. One way of increasing the seasonal attraction of a woody shrub or small tree is to grow a second plant, a climbing or trailing one, through it. Choose a specimen to complement the colours of the host plant, whether it flowers at the same time as its host or separately, and one that will neither outgrow nor overwhelm the host.

By using the full range of plants available – trees, shrubs, climbers, herbaceous perennials, annuals and bulbs – it is possible to have colour in every season of the year. Then, even if the weather prevents work or relaxation outside, the garden still looks attractive through the window. Seeing flowers in the depths of winter has a cheering effect, and proves that spring really isn't that far away.

Strong foliage can look spectacular in winter, when frost highlights the sharply toothed leaves of plants such as *Helleborus argutifolius* and mahonia, or makes the seed-heads of bronze fennel sparkle in the early mist. Birds appreciate the berries on plants like pyracantha, which persist on the plant throughout the winter if they are allowed.

Plant at all levels to make full use of the space. If the foliage of a herbaceous plant dies off in the autumn and does not return until late spring, fill the gap with early-flowering bulbs or corms, such as cyclamen (*C. hederifolium* or *C. coum*), crocus, snowdrop, dwarf narcissus, or dwarf iris, which will flower and die down again before the larger plant needs the room. They can be left in place throughout the year, even in a container, so that there is no root disturbance to plants nearby.

Above: Monarda *'Croftway Pink'* gives a beautiful show of colour in the autumn.

Above: *Colours in a summer scheme can be hot and vibrant or pale and cooling.*

Opposite: *Autumn flowers and foliage are complemented by orange gourds.*

PLANTS FOR YEAR-ROUND COLOUR

Winter
Cyclamen coum
Garrya elliptica 'James Roof'
Helleborus orientalis
Iris unguicularis
Mahonia x *media* 'Charity'

Spring
Berberis darwinii
Bergenia cordifolia
Forsythia 'Fiesta'
Galanthus nivalis
  (snowdrop)
Primula auricula

Summer
Deutzia 'Mont Rose'
Geranium sanguineum
Lilium
Lonicera x *brownii*
  'Dropmore Scarlet'
Lysimachia punctata

Autumn
Clematis orientalis
  'Bill MacKenzie'
Coreopsis verticillata
  'Grandiflora'
Escallonia 'Iveyi'
Hypericum x *moserianum*
Monarda 'Croftway Pink'

Edible Planting

Vegetable-growing isn't the first project that springs to mind for the balcony or roof gardener but, in fact, there is a lot of scope for making the most of even a tiny gardening space to produce fruit, vegetables and herbs for the table. The taste of food brought in and eaten fresh from the garden is better than any bought from the shops, and, even in a small area, there are plenty of varieties that can be grown.

DWARF VARIETIES

Many fruit varieties are available on a dwarfing rootstock, which keeps them small, and they can be grown in containers, either as normally shaped trees, or as single-stemmed cordons. Against a warm wall, fan-shaped peaches, nectarines and cherries will thrive, as will grapes, which can also be grown over a pergola.

A new generation of "mini-vegetables" have been bred that are aimed at the smaller growing area and designed to be harvested and eaten while they are still small and tender. Tomatoes, cucumbers, aubergines (eggplants) and peppers will all thrive in containers, as long as they are sheltered.

Herbs, particularly the more ornamental ones, such as purple basil (*Ocimum basilicum* 'Dark Opal') and variegated sages and mints, are decorative as well as useful. Edible flowers, such as nasturtiums, pot marigolds and borage, can be added to salads or frozen into ice cubes to add to summer drinks.

The main requirements for a successful crop are sunshine, water, food and shelter from cold winds. Sun is needed to ripen the fruit and keep the more tender crops, such as courgettes (zucchini), aubergines and peaches, at a warm enough temperature. Most edible plants need a lot of water. This is especially important for plants such as tomatoes, whose fruit has a high water content when ripe.

Edible plants may also need a soil or compost (soil mix) which is rich in organic matter or fertilizer, to provide the nutrients for their rapid growth, although the amount needed does vary from variety to variety, with lettuces being far more dependent on water than food, for example. For this reason, a crop of tomatoes in a grow-bag can be followed the next year by a crop of lettuce and radishes grown in the same bag.

MINIATURE KITCHEN GARDEN

1 Not many of us have the space or time to maintain a kitchen garden, but this table-top selection will allow you to grow all the essentials. Place crocks in the bottom of terracotta pots for drainage. Plants with well-developed root systems, such as this marigold, will benefit from planting in a larger pot.

2 Pots of basil and other herbs are available from garden centres and many supermarkets. They can be potted on successfully to provide fresh herbs throughout the season. You may be able to divide a single plant into two or more pots when repotting.

3 Nasturtiums flower better in poor soil, and once planted should be left to their own devices. Give them a little water but no plant food or you will get lots of leaves and no flowers.

4 Additional plants to grow might include miniature tomato and strawberry plants. They need larger pots to allow for root development. Line a tray with a thick plastic sheet and cover with clay granules. These retain moisture and create a damp microclimate for the plants.

Left: *Many fruit varieties such as redcurrants can be grown in small spaces or pots.*

Above: *Tomatoes are easy to grow in small spaces. Ensure the plants, especially when situated on a balcony or roof terrace, are adequately protected from strong winds.*

Right: *Position your miniature garden in a sheltered area, preferably as near to the kitchen as possible, to enjoy produce all summer long.*

Maintenance for Balconies and Roof Gardens

Keeping the balcony or roof garden in a good condition will enhance your enjoyment of it. You need to consider the structure, the plants, and the fixtures and fittings. The big advantage of the balcony and roof garden over the ground-level variety is that many of the back-breaking routine tasks, such as digging, are simply not necessary. However, other jobs are unique to these areas and mustn't be neglected.

PLANTS
In general, the plants will need weeding only if any seedlings happen to appear, and pruning only to keep them healthy and in shape. If any are tied against a wall, check the wires and nails periodically, to make sure they are not pulling away, and tie in new shoots. Occasionally, especially if the plants are protected from the rain, wipe any build-up of dust from the leaves; if dust is allowed to remain, it will interfere with photosynthesis, and the growth of the plant will be slower. As a matter of routine, remove dead leaves from the plants before they begin to rot.

FLOOR SURFACES
The balcony is probably the easiest to maintain, because, by its very nature as an extended part of the living area, it is usually easy to sweep clean or wash down.

Decking will need to be brushed with a stiff brush to remove any algae; then treat with an algae killer. In addition, treat softwood decks with a preservative every year.

Wash tiles periodically to reduce any build-up of algae; re-lay any tiles that work loose before they crack.

Concrete tends to suffer most damage from small cracks. If you overlook or ignore these, the action of the weather, or a stray seedling that grows in the crack, can enlarge it and cause considerable damage. Chip away loose material and repair the hole with a stiff mixture of concrete containing an adhesive.

Regularly rake any gravel level; it should not need any other attention.

Left: *Many herbaceous plants look better if dead-headed, but large-flowered shrubs benefit as well. With shrubs, be careful to remove only the dead flower in case you inadvertently remove the buds for the shoots carrying next year's flowers.*

Below: *Maintain deck floors by brushing and washing down with an anti-algae treatment.*

Railings

Rub these down and repaint them with a weather-resistant paint when they show signs of damage.

Electrical Fittings

If electricity has been connected to the roof garden, for lights or a pond pump, it should be checked every year for signs of wear; this is best done by a qualified electrician, who can replace any damaged cables or connections.

Left: Wooden furniture should be treated with wood preservative at the end of each season. Hardwood furniture needs little care but will benefit from being cleaned and oiled.

Below: Most containers will need little looking after but do check for signs of cracking before replanting in the spring.

Seating

Bring the cushions from upholstered furniture inside during wet or cold weather and clean them according to the instructions. Wash plastic frames with a detergent solution periodically to remove the water marks left by rain.

Metal furniture can be left outside but it will need a scrub in spring with a detergent solution, to remove the dust and deposits of the winter. It will benefit from a new coat of weather-resistant paint every two or three years.

Treat softwood timber seating with a preservative or new coat of varnish every year. Hardwoods, such as teak, do not need preservative. A rub over with white spirit, soap and water and, finally, teak oil will protect them for the year.

Containers

Most containers will need little maintenance. Weathering tends to enhance their appearance rather than detract from it. Any that have been painted may need another coat, and reconstituted stone containers may need to be brushed down.

Trellises and Pergolas

Particularly where the trellis has been erected as a windbreak, the means of support will need regular checking to make sure it is still rigidly in place. The bottoms of posts are prone to rot. Treat them with preservative but, as many wood treatments are toxic to plants, it is usually better to detach the plants from their supports, and protect them before you begin applying the preservative.

CHOOSING PLANTS

Buying Plants

Before making the journey to select plants for your garden make sure you have a clear idea of where you are going to plant them, the type of soil and the aspect of your garden. Read the label and examine the plant before you buy it to make sure it is right for the spot you have in mind. Buying the wrong plant could waste a whole growing season.

USE AND SEASON OF INTEREST

Before buying a plant, it is worth considering where it is to go in the garden – especially if it is an impulse buy. It is said that a keen gardener can always find room for one more plant, but that does rather depend on the size of the plant in question.

Always check the plant's label for information about final height and spread – and how many years it will take to grow to full size – and ask for help if the label doesn't tell you. Then consider the situation you have in mind for the plant and whether the fully grown specimen will be in scale and in keeping with its surroundings.

Be sure to check when the main season of interest is, or whether it has the added bonus of a second one. The plant has not yet been discovered which can be interesting in all four seasons of the year, but many evergreen variegated plants, such as *Elaeagnus* x *ebbingei* 'Gilt Edge', do come close to it. This shrub has bright golden-yellow markings on leaves which are retained on the plant throughout the year and do not easily

succumb to weather damage. *Cotinus coggygria* 'Royal Purple' is a tall, handsome shrub that, though leafless during the winter, has fluffy pink flowers in summer and rich plum-purple leaves throughout the spring and summer, which turn a dazzling red colour in autumn before they fall. The small, upright flowering cherry tree, *Prunus* 'Amanogawa', produces masses of soft pink flowers in spring and a spectacular show of colour in autumn, as the leaves turn to fiery reds, oranges and yellows, making the tree resemble a bright flame.

It is important that any plant earns its keep, but nowhere more so than in a smaller garden, where space is at a premium.

Left: *Adding organic matter to the soil will encourage earthworms, which will in turn improve the condition of the soil.*

SITE PREFERENCES

Every plant has a preference for the ideal conditions it needs in order to grow well, whether it is hot or shady, acid or alkaline, dry or damp, and most will have the greatest of difficulty growing in the wrong position.

Many conditions can be modified, at least to some extent, to extend the range of plants which can be grown. Improve the drainage of a localized wet spot, for example, by incorporating sharp sand or gravel into the soil, and by adding organic matter, such as well-rotted farmyard manure, to encourage worm activity. Dry areas will also benefit from the addition of organic

Above: *Gravel incorporated into a localized wet area will improve drainage.*

matter, which will hold moisture during the vital summer months, and also from the use of a mulch over the surface, to reduce the amount of moisture lost by evaporation and reduce competition from weeds.

Acidic conditions can be modified by the addition of ground limestone or chalk, to raise the pH. It is difficult to lower the pH if the soil is alkaline, however. Flowers of sulphur will have some effect on alkalinity but the difference is only very slight and you will have to repeat the treatment every year. On the whole, it is better to choose plants that will thrive in your soil rather than labouring to change its pH, which may involve a lot of effort for little reward; a great range of plants will not mind a slight alkalinity. You will have to settle for growing acid-lovers in containers, and this is very successful and suitable for many of them. Many fascinating and attractive plants also enjoy growing in acidic conditions, so choose wisely and watch your plants thrive.

SIZE AND SHAPE

In the days when plants were grown and sold by the nurseryman, it was easy to ask advice about the plant being bought and its ultimate dimensions. These days, most plants are bought from large, impersonal garden centres, and so the label that accompanies them is all-important. Now that labelling plants is largely a computerized process, it should, theoretically, be difficult to make a mistake; judging by the number of cedars (*Cedrus atlantica* 'Glauca' in particular) still being planted in small front gardens, however, mistakes do still happen. There are very few truly small trees, although there are many that can be classified as "slow-growing" and that may take 50 years to reach a size that causes difficulties.

Right: *Dwarf conifers are a good choice in a small garden as they will mature without becoming a danger to near-by buildings.*

Looking at Healthy Plants

Once you have established what plants will thrive in the conditions in your garden, you can prepare to make your selection with confidence. There are certain signs to look out for to ensure you are choosing a healthy specimen.

PLANT HEALTH

Take a good look at the plant before buying it to inspect it for signs of pests, disease or damage. Start with the leaves, which should be free from holes, bitten edges, wiggly patterns across the middle, yellow patches (unless it is variegated!) or brown spots. Leaves should feel firm and should not flop down. Stems should also feel firm, with no signs of being eaten, and no small, oval, brown bumps (scale insects) on them. Occasionally, a woody plant will suffer a snapped twig in transit; as long as it is trimmed off cleanly and quickly, this should not pose a problem. Look for signs of fungal attack, particularly the tiny coral-coloured spots of *Nectria cinnabarina*, a fungus that will

Above: *This plant is suffering from whitefly, which look like tiny white moths and often rise up in a cloud when disturbed. They can be controlled with any recommended contact insecticide.*

attack both live and dead wood and can easily kill a young plant.

The surface of the compost (soil mix) in the pot is a good indicator of the length of time the plant has been in the garden centre and, therefore, how long it has been in the same pot. If the compost is covered with weed seedlings, moss or liverwort, it has spent some time in the same place and is likely to be under-nourished.

The plant may also be pot-bound, a condition in which the roots, having nowhere to go as they grow, end up circling round and round inside the pot. The plant may find it hard to break this habit, leading to a poorly anchored plant that will be susceptible to being blown over

Above: *Aphids are the best-known plant pests. Greenfly and blackfly are the common ones, but there are many species, some affecting the roots of plants rather than the leaves.*

in a high wind. The roots of a healthy plant will be fat and swollen, and white, yellow or chestnut-brown, but they should not be shrivelled or dark brown. Don't be afraid to knock the plant out of its pot to inspect the roots.

Often, newly potted plants are on sale alongside ones from previous deliveries that have not sold; younger ones will establish much more quickly, even if they are slightly smaller to start with. Don't be fooled – biggest is not best in the world of plants!

WHERE TO BUY PLANTS

Plants are sold in different places, from supermarkets to nurseries, and they will have received different levels of care.

Those sold on the same site where they were raised are likely to be younger and healthier than those which had to endure a journey to their destination. As they are transported, plants may undergo a period of drought, which will affect their growth.

Conditions at the point of sale also affect the health of plants: on a roadside or garage forecourt they are exposed to drying winds, high or low temperatures and pollution; in a supermarket, the watering might be erratic and the lighting poor. Plants in a garden centre should be well cared for in terms of watering and temperature, although the longer they remain unsold, the more they will begin to suffer as the reserve of slow-release fertilizer in their pot runs out.

Nurseries are a good choice for specialized and more unusual plants, and expert advice on choosing and caring for them. The selection in garden centres is improving and they stock a wide range of different types of plant. Generally, centres that look after their plants will often also take trouble with labelling and advice.

Below: *Some commercial growers supply plants mail order. These fuchsias have been dispatched in lightweight but highly protective packages, and the quality of the plants is high.*

TECHNIQUES

Mulching

Mulches can be used to help improve growing conditions for plants. An effective mulch should reduce weeds and the amount of moisture lost through evaporation.

A weed can be defined as "a plant out of place" and any such plant will compete directly with the plants that are supposed to be there, for light, moisture and nutrients. Seeds contain a limited amount of food and the further the seedling has to grow before it reaches the surface, the more likely it is that its food will run out before it gets there. To give your seedlings a fighting chance, an organic mulch needs to be at least 10cm (4in) thick to give total weed suppression.

The main advantages of organic mulches are that they look attractive, can often be home-made (and are therefore inexpensive), and are gradually incorporated into the soil by the activity of worms, adding to the organic-matter content. They do need topping up every year to remain effective.

Inorganic mulches, such as black plastic and woven membranes, are less pleasing to the eye but provide a much more effective barrier against weeds. It is possible to use a combination of both types. Lay the artificial material, then cover with an even layer of bark or gravel. This creates the best of both worlds, providing good protection against weeds and a pleasing appearance in the garden.

Above: *Around a flower or shrub border, where appearance matters, cover any bare ground or plastic sheeting with a layer of bark chips or other decorative mulch.*

Staking Plants

Staking or supporting plants as they grow will keep the garden looking tidy. This can be done in such a way that the supports blend in with the rest of the garden.

There are different types of support, from metal, plastic and timber frames to wooden stakes and plastic-coated wires. Informal supports include canes, woven hurdles, raffia and string.

Whichever means of support you choose, place it in position by, or over, the plant early in the season, because it is a great deal easier to guide the stems through the frame as they grow than to try to poke them through it once they are long and liable to damage. If you do this, the foliage will grow to cover the frame and, by the time the plant actually needs it, the support will be almost invisible.

1 Proprietary supports are very efficient at supporting border plants that are not very tall but have a mass of tallish floppy or fragile flowering stems.

2 Twiggy sticks pushed into the ground around the plants can be very effective. They may look unsightly initially, but will blend in with the surroundings more easily than artificial supports.

3 Short canes can be used to support plants such as carnations. If you use a stout cane, loop string or twine around it and the plant. Use thinner split canes to keep individual flower stems upright.

Feeding Plants

Giving plants sufficient nutrients will ensure strong growth, abundant flowering and fruit production, and make them healthy enough to withstand pests and diseases.

BALANCED NUTRIENTS

In common with all living things, plants need a balanced intake of nutrients to survive. These take the form of minerals and trace elements, which all have a part to play in keeping the plant healthy. In their natural environment these would be available in the soil, to be taken up, along with water, by the roots. They are then transported within the plant to supply the leaf cells, where the process of photosynthesis manufactures sugars and starches – which are also essential for a healthy plant – from the sunlight. As the plant grows, flowers and eventually dies, the decaying material then releases nutrients back into the soil.

In the garden, where far more plants are grown closely together than would happen in nature, the competition for nutrients becomes intense; this is exacerbated if the plant is in a container, where the roots cannot grow into new areas in search of extra food.

Seaweed

TYPES OF FERTILIZER

There are two groups of fertilizer: organic and inorganic. The organic ones are derived from natural ingredients, such as other plants (seaweed or nettles), blood, fish or bone, and generally last longer, although they tend to become available to the plant only slowly after application. Inorganic fertilizers are mineral-based and break down more quickly after application.

Growmore

The rate at which the fertilizer is released into the soil depends on temperature, soil-organism activity, the fertilizer's solubility in water and its size (the finer the particles, the more quickly they will be absorbed). Some fertilizers are called "controlled-release", which means that the particles are surrounded by a soluble coating which has a breakdown period of a number of months. The nutrients are released gradually to the plant; after this more fertilizer will be needed.

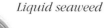

Liquid seaweed

Blood, fish and bone

Those fertilizers which are applied as a liquid are released to and absorbed by the plants the most quickly of all (within 5–7 days), and are useful as a fast-acting tonic if a plant is looking ill. This is especially true of foliar feeds, which are applied directly to the leaves rather than the soil around the roots, and are absorbed straight into the plant's system. These can have an effect within 3–4 days, compared with up to 21 days for a general granular fertilizer applied around the roots.

Nitro phosphate

Nitro chalk

THE N:P:K RATIO

On the back of the pack of fertilizer, there should be some information about the nutrients it contains, the three most important elements being nitrogen (N), phosphorus (P) and potassium (K). Nitrogen promotes healthy growth of leaves and shoots, phosphorus is needed for healthy root development and potassium improves flowering and fruit production. Put simply, N:P:K equals shoots:roots:fruits. The ratio is given on the pack because certain plants need some elements in a greater quantity than others – a foliage plant, for instance, will need more nitrogen and less potassium, as it produces leaves but not a great show of flowers or fruit, whereas tomatoes need huge quantities of potassium to give a good yield. It is often necessary to change the fertilizer through the season, particularly for heavy feeders like vegetables. Apply more nitrogen and phosphorus in the spring to promote growth, and increase potassium as the season progresses, in order to produce a good show of flowers or fruit.

Fishmeal

Sulphate of ammonia

Applying Fertilizer

Even if fertilizer is only applied to the garden once a year it is worth the effort because as well as making the plants look good, a balanced supply of nutrients also helps them to fight off attacks of pests and diseases.

BENEFITS

Pests and diseases cause the plant stress and, while a healthy plant can often shrug off an attack, a plant that is already suffering may well die.

In an established garden, you can apply fertilizer in granular form as a dressing around the plants early in the season, or in soluble form as the plants are watered during the spring. For a new plant, mix fertilizer with the soil as it is replaced in the planting hole around the rootball. Lawns will benefit from dressings of mixed weed-killer and fertilizer in the spring and autumn, keeping the grass healthy, and helping fight the effects of any dry periods in summer and cold spells in winter.

Slow-release fertilizer

Dried manure

FEEDING BEDS AND BORDERS

1 Most established plants, benefit from annual feeding. Apply a slow- or controlled-release fertilizer in spring or early summer, sprinkling it around the bushes. Keep it away from the stem, sprinkling it out further where most of the active root growth is.

2 Hoe it into the surface so that it penetrates the root area more quickly.

3 Unless rain is expected, water it in. This will make the fertilizer active more quickly in dry conditions.

FEEDING THE LAWN

1 The quickest way to feed your lawn is with a wheeled spreader. Although individual models vary, you can usually adjust the delivery rate. Test the rate on a measured area of path first, then sweep up the fertilizer and weigh it to make sure the application rate is correct.

2 An easy way to give your lawn a liquid boost is to use a sprinkler system into which you can introduce special fertilizer pellets. It will feed the lawn as it waters.

3 A hose-ended sprayer like this is a good way to apply a soluble fertilizer for a quick response. You can use this type of hose-ended sprayer for beds and borders as well as for the lawn.

Weeds in Lawns

A weedy lawn will spoil the overall look of your garden, but with modern weedkillers it is easy to eliminate weeds. The method below ensures a weed-free lawn with as little as one application a year.

1 Weeds in lawns are best controlled by a selective hormone weedkiller, ideally applied in mid- or late spring. These are usually applied as a liquid, using a dribble bar attached to a watering can. To ensure even application you should mark out lines with string, spacing them about the width of the dribble bar apart.

2 Always mix and apply weedkiller as recommended by the manufacturer. There are a number of different plant hormones used, some killing certain weeds better than others, so always check that it is recommended for the weeds you want to control. When mixed simply walk along each strip slowly enough for the droplets from the dribble bar to cover the area evenly.

3 If your lawn also needs feeding you can save time by using a combined weed-and-feed. The most efficient way to apply these – which are likely to be granular rather than liquid – is with a fertilizer spreader.

4 If you have just a few troublesome spots in a small area you will not need to treat the whole lawn. A spot weeder that you dab or wipe into the weed will work well.

Weeds in Beds and Borders

As mentioned previously, mulches are an organic means of preventing weed growth. Herbicides can also be used if you are careful in your application.

CHEMICAL SOLUTIONS

Although there are weedkillers that will kill some problem grasses growing among broad-leaved plants, generally you cannot use selective weedkillers in beds and borders as they will kill or damage whatever plants they come into contact with. There are ways you can use herbicides around ornamental plants to cut down on the amount of hand-weeding needed.

1 In borders, deep-rooted perennial "problem" weeds, such as bindweed, are best treated by painting on a translocated weedkiller such as one based on glyphosate. Ordinary contact weedkillers may not kill all the roots, but this chemical is moved by the plant to all parts. Even so, you may have to treat really troublesome weeds a number of times. Use a gel formulation to paint on where watering the weedkillers may cause damage to adjacent plants.

2 You may be able to treat areas in a shrub border with watered-on weedkiller simply by shielding the cultivated plants. If deep-rooted perennials are not a problem you can use a contact weedkiller that will act like a chemical hoe. A real hoe may be an easier alternative to mixing and applying a weedkiller if the area is small.

3 Once the ground is clear, if you don't want to use a mulch, try applying a weedkiller intended to prevent new seedlings from emerging. These are only suitable for certain shrubs and fruit crops, but they remain near the surface above root level and only act on seedlings that try to germinate. These should suppress most new weeds for many months.

Preparing the Ground

Your plants have a much better chance of successful growth if you give them the best start in life by preparing the ground thoroughly before planting out.

Planting Trees

If you choose your species wisely, bearing in mind its size when fully grown, even the smallest garden can usually incorporate a small or dwarf variety.

1 Before planting, prepare the ground by digging over the area at least a month before planting. This will allow the soil to settle and weed seedlings to germinate.

2 Dig out any deep-rooted perennial weeds that appear. Hoe out the seedlings and rake level. Water all the plants in their pots first, and then set them out in their intended positions.

3 Knock the plants from their pots and tease out a few roots if they are running tightly around the edge of the pot. Plant at their original depth, and firm the soil around the roots before planting the next one.

4 Water the ground thoroughly and keep well watered for the first season.

1 When planting in lawns, mark out the edge of a circular bed with sand. Push the spade in vertically around the edge first, then push the spade in at a shallow angle to lift the turf.

2 Remove the top 30 cm (12 in) of soil, then fork over the rest thoroughly, working in plenty of garden compost or well-rotted manure.

3 Before you plant the tree, insert a stake, placing it on the side of the prevailing wind. Hammer it in, allowing sufficient space for the rootball. Then tease out some of the roots of the tree.

4 Place the roots in the soil, checking that the soil mark on the tree's stem is level with the ground. Fill the hole with soil and tread it down firmly. Water and apply a mulch to conserve moisture. Fix the tree to the stake with a tree tie.

Multiplying Plants

The results will not be as quick as would be gained by buying more plants, but you will ultimately achieve complete ground cover at a fraction of the cost.

1 Some shrubby ground-cover plants that spread by underground runners or suckers (such as *Pachysandra terminalis*) can be easily divided into smaller pieces. A plant like this can be divided into three or four plants. Water first to make sure the compost (potting mix) is moist.

2 Knock the plant out of its pot. If it doesn't pull out easily, try tapping the edge of the pot on a hard surface.

3 Carefully pull the rootball apart, trying to keep as much compost on the roots as possible.

4 If you find the crown too tough to pull apart, try cutting through it with a knife. It is better to do this than damage the plant even more if it does not separate easily.

5 It has been possible to divide this plant into eight smaller ones, but the number you will be able to achieve depends on the size of the original plant and the species.

6 Replant immediately if you don't mind smaller plants, otherwise pot up and grow on for a year before planting.

7 Pot up the plants if you want to grow them on, using a good compost. Keep them in a sheltered but light position, and make sure they are never short of water.

8 If you don't have automatic watering, plunge the pots up to their rims in soil. They will dry out less quickly and watering will not be such a chore.

Pruning

Whether it is to improve the shape of a plant, to make it produce more flowers or fruit, or to correct some damage, pruning is an important part of the procedure for maintaining the health of many plants.

Below: *Shrubs such as rhododendrons are grown on a rootstock that is decoratively inferior to the variety grafted on to it. Often, the rootstock will try to re-establish itself and* *suckers will appear. Remove the suckers as close to the ground as possible to ensure that the superior flowers of the grafted shrub will not be taken over by the new shrub.*

BENEFITS OF PRUNING

Most plants will benefit from pruning at some time during their life. Regular dead-heading for annuals, for example, if they are not required to set seed, is essential for a good display of flowers and to prolong the flowering season to the maximum. Because you remove the fading flowers, the plant does not waste energy producing seed (after which it is likely to die down) and devotes itself to producing more flowers.

For harder pruning, use a sharp, clean knife or secateurs (pruners) to remove certain sections. This allows buds further back down the plant to develop as replacements for the ones you have cut off, and these can be trained to grow in the desired direction. Normally, the bud that develops on the shoot will be the one at the tip – a characteristic know as "apical dominance" – caused by the stronger concentration of plant hormones in the tip bud, which suppresses the ones behind. If this apical bud is removed by pruning, the other buds will develop to replace it, causing much more branching than would otherwise have been the case. The gardener can capitalize on this tendency to encourage the plant to become bushier.

In general, most "hard" pruning is done on woody plants, with bedding, annuals and herbaceous perennials needing dead-heading.

REASONS FOR PRUNING

On some plants, pruning is an annual procedure, carried out to keep the plant to a suitable size or to encourage it to produce larger flowers, more fruit or better coloured stems. On others, it is an operation carried out occasionally, perhaps as a result of damage, to prevent the open wound becoming infected and harming the plant. As a matter of routine, every plant should be checked regularly for signs of the "three Ds" – disease, damage and death. If a diseased branch is caught early, and pruned back to uninfected wood, there is less chance of the problem infecting the rest of the plant. Areas of damage expose the tissue underneath the bark, and are ideal sites for fungal spores and diseases to enter the plant. Dead branches can also act as hosts to fungi and diseases, some of which can easily travel into the living tissue and damage it. Any suspect shoots should be pruned back to clean, healthy tissue as soon as possible, using clean equipment.

TYPES OF PRUNING

The main types of pruning are:
• Formative pruning, when the plant is young, to encourage the development of a strong framework of branches.
• Containment pruning, where, as the plant ages, it is regularly pruned in order to keep its size and shape within the constraints of the garden.

Below: *This well-formed floribunda rose has plenty of new, vigorous, even growth and an abundance of flowers.*

• Remedial pruning, when the "three Ds" rule is put into operation, to maintain the health of the plant. Remedial pruning is also used to eliminate any crossing or congested branches and, on variegated shrubs, to remove any shoots which have reverted to plain green (variegated shoots are weaker than green ones, as they contain slightly less chlorophyll, so that if the green ones are if left in place, the whole plant will revert).

TIMING

Timing the pruning operation correctly is critical to the performance of the plant; if you prune at the wrong time, you may cut off all the flower buds for the season. Not all plants can be pruned for the year in early spring; in fact, the best time to prune many, especially flowering shrubs, is right after they have flowered, so that they have the maximum time to develop their buds for the following season.

FORMATIVE PRUNING FOR SHRUBS

1 The best time to prune shrubs is as soon as possible after the flowers have faded.

2 Shorten the growth from the last summer by half. It will be paler and more supple than than older wood.

3 Avoid cutting into dark, older wood as new shoots are seldom produced from this.

4 From a distance the difference after pruning will not be obvious but it should be neater and more compact. The real benefit will be cumulative. Remember to start pruning while the plant is still young.

CONTAINMENT PRUNING FOR SHRUBS

1 These old stems show how much growth can be made in a season on a plant that was pruned the previous spring. Some of the dead flower heads are still visible.

2 Simply cut back all the previous summer's growth to within about 5cm (2in) of last year's stem. Do not worry if this seems drastic. The plant will soon produce vigorous new shoots and replace the ones you are cutting out.

3 Cut back to just above a bud. Keep to outward-facing buds as much as possible to give a bushier effect. Most of the shoots should be cut back to within about 5cm (2in) of the base of last year's growth, but if the bush is very old and congested, cut out one or two stems close to ground level. This will prevent stems rubbing against each other, and improve air circulation.

4 This is what a plant that has been cut back to a low framework of old stems looks like. Try to keep the height after pruning about 90cm (3ft) or less.

PRUNING A NEGLECTED HEDGE

1 A hedge or screen that becomes too tall or wide can take up valuable garden space, and it will make hedge trimming more of a chore. It is sometimes possible to reduce the width of an old hedge by drastic pruning spread over a couple of seasons, and it is often possible to reduce its height radically. Tackle one side the first year and the other side the following year, by which time the first side should be growing vigorously. Saw the branches back to a point less than the final desired width. Allow space for the new growth that will be necessary to clothe the stumps after pruning.

2 The thickness of the shoots at the centre of an old hedge will probably preclude the use of secateurs (pruners) or even long-handled pruners (loppers). A pruning saw is an efficient way to deal with these thick shoots. On shoots that are thin enough, however, use secateurs or long-handled pruners as these are much quicker than sawing.

3 New growth should appear from the stumps, although some plants shoot from old wood more readily than others. Trim this new growth back when it is about 15cm (6in) long to encourage bushy growth, then gradually allow it to extend to the desired width. This hedge has been reduced in height and width and is now much more manageable.

PRUNING A NEW HEDGE

1 If you buy plants sold specifically for hedging they are likely to be young plants with probably a straight single stem. These keep the cost down, but formative pruning is particularly important to ensure that they make bushy plants. Plants like this privet should be cut back to about 15cm (6in) to stimulate low branching.

2 New shoots will be produced if you shorten the main (leading) shoot after planting. Trim these back by about half in early or midsummer.

3 Some hedging plants will be bushier when you buy them, like the ones shown here. Shorten the height of these plants by one-third.

4 Do not remove the main (leading) shoot of a conifer, large-leaved evergreens such as aucuba or laurel, or beech or hornbeam. Trim that off only when the hedge is approaching the desired height. Shorten other shoots by between one-quarter and one-third, to stimulate bushy growth.

PRUNING WINTER DAMAGE

PRUNING VARIEGATED PLANTS

1 Shrubs of borderline hardiness may be damaged but not killed by a cold winter.

2 In spring cut out cold-damaged shoots. Often you need to remove the affected tip only. This will improve the appearance and new growth will soon hide the gaps.

3 Once the damaged shoots have been removed the shrub will recover.

1 Check variegated plants to make sure they are not "reverting" (producing shoots with all green leaves). If you leave these on the plant they will gradually dominate it because they are normally more vigorous. Cut them back to their point of origin.

Page numbers in italic
refer to illustrations

PICTURE CREDITS

A–Z Botanical: pp 75 right (© Moira Newman), 74 bottom right,
75 left (© Simon Butcher).
Jonathan Buckley: pp 12 top left, 12 top right, 12 bottom left;
14 bottom right, 15 left, 15 right, 16 bottom left, 16 top right, 16 centre,
16 right, 17 top left, 18, 20 top right, 33, 34 bottom left, 34 centre, 42, 43, 52
bottom left, 56, 57, 58, 66 bottom left, 66 bottom right, 76 bottom left.
Camera Press: pp 11, 50 (© Linda Burgess), 55, 73 (© Linda Burgess), 74.
John Freeman: pp 13, 26 bottom left, 59 bottom right, 62, 70, 72,
78 right, 80, 84, 85, 87.
Garden Picture Library: pp 10 top right, 30 bottom left, 35,
66 top (© Steven Wooster), 71 (© Friedrich Strauss),
74 top right (© Ron Sutherland/garden design: Duane Paul Design Team),
76 top right, 77 (© Friedrich Strauss).
Michelle Garrett: p 54 top.
Harry Smith Horticultural Collection: pp 19, 53.
Jacqui Hurst: pp 78 bottom left, 79 left.
Debbie Patterson: pp 30 top right, 51 bottom left, 63.
Robert Harding Picture Library: p 81 (© Niall McDiarmid).
Juliette Wade: pp 7, 8, 12 bottom right, 16 bottom right, 17 bottom right,
20 bottom left, 21, 22, 23 top right, 24, 26 top, 26 right, 27, 28, 29, 31,
34 top right, 36, 37, 38, 39, 40, 41, 44, 45, 46, 51 top right, 54 bottom left,
59 bottom left, 61.